The
Book
of
Visions

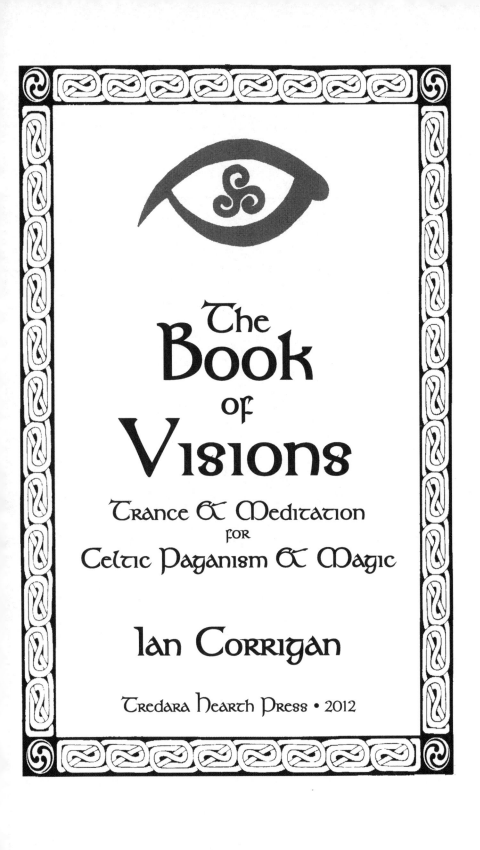

The
Book
of
Visions

Trance & Meditation
for
Celtic Paganism & Magic

Ian Corrigan

Tredara Hearth Press • 2012

The Book of Visions

Dedicated to the
Lord of Wisdom
&
To my Priestess
Liafal

Book of Visions - Table of Contents

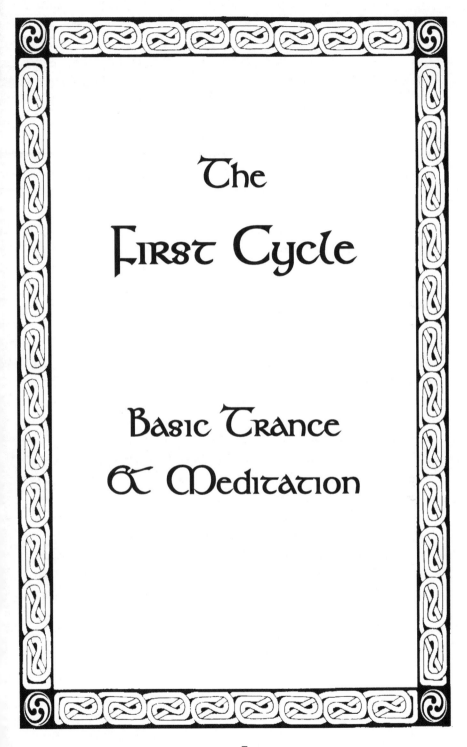

The
First Cycle

Basic Trance
& Meditation

The First Cycle - Training the Mind

The work of magic is the work of disciplining the mind, body and spirit to serve the will of the magician. In this we place the Will at the crown of the human psycho-structure. Deep in the jungle of our neural network, where the electrochemical lightning flashes information between tentacled synapses there lurks that undiscovered source from which the free will of mortals arises. Unproven by material science, it is known to the Wise as the Will, the divine source that makes each being, each individual manifestation of the chaos foam, able to act directly in and upon the Web of the Worlds.

Meditation is the work of the Will. Through cultivating relaxed, calm concentration we learn to stand above the internal weather of our minds. To enter Basic Trance may feel like a step away from will, but in fact it is a step away from the chattering programmed mind and body, toward a quiet that allows the Will to become directly active. Without devolving into doctrine, it should be said that the apparent self, the personality construct, is a robot of emotional habits, fixed opinions and programmed physical responses. That robot has often been considered the opponent of art, and magic, and spirit. To gain skill in meditation and trance is to gain access to the controls of the robot, and to expand awareness outside our common selves.

In the work of magical art we are often asked to inflame the passions. We praise our own names, and array ourselves in light. We penetrate behind common appearances, into misty lanes and unmarked territory. We encounter Gods who arouse high and wild excitement, we walk in dark places where we may meet our fears. The very best protection against error in such practices is skill in meditation.

I advise every student of magic to take up the work of training in this skill. While the exercises offered here are enough to develop basic skill, I have found that even a small number of experiences with a live teacher can allow faster and more effective learning of the basics. There are also a number of recorded instructions that may be useful to some people.

By whatever method, do not neglect these basic skills as you seek the wonders of the Inner Worlds.

Part 1: Basic Trance & Meditation

Basic Trance

What modern mind-skill refers to as basic trance is simple enough. It is a combination of physical calmness and relaxation with intensely focused concentration of attention and a commitment to set aside doubt and self-critique during the exercise. Together these produce a relaxed, focused awareness that is ready to be worked with by the personal will. This is the basic state in which to begin ritual, the preliminary state from which more specific types are meditation are launched. This state is both simple to begin with and able to be deepened almost indefinitely by practice.

• The Complete Breath

The Wise know that to control the breath is to control the mind. To begin, sit comfortably, with your spine straight. Your tailbone should be higher than your ankles, your hands resting loosely on your lap or on the arms of your chair. Your eyes may be slightly open, or closed. You then begin a pattern of rhythmic breathing.

Proper breath comes from the diaphragm. When you inhale, your lower abdomen should expand, as though you were pulling air into the bottom of the lungs. Then fill the rest of the lungs, expanding the chest. When the breath is held, do not close the throat. Keep the diaphragm and chest expanded to let the air rest in the lungs. Exhaling reverses the process, emptying the chest then raising the diaphragm by pressing the belly toward the backbone. Again, the breath is held out of the body by the muscles of the chest and belly, not by closing the throat.

Tradition offers several patterns for rhythm of the breath. Many people like the classic 4/4 pattern - in for four beats, hold for four beats, out for four beats, hold for four beats. The speed of the rhythm is up to you. A little practice will allow you to find a pace that is comfortable, neither too slow nor too fast. Some prefer a pattern with shorter holds, perhaps in-4, hold-2, out-4, hold-2.

If you are beginning meditation, your daily practice can be the practice of the Complete Breath, perhaps practiced as a preliminary to your devotions, until it is habitual and comfortable. You will find that it shades naturally into the core techniques of trance and meditation.

• Progressive Deep Relaxation

This exercise is, in essence, a set of calisthenics for your body and mind. It is intended to induce a deeper state of relaxation than normal, and provide the chance to observe and remember that state. A full exercise of this sort isn't a part of ritual practice, rather it is a training method, by which relaxation becomes a familiar response. Once that relaxation is induced and remembered, it becomes much easier to focus and settle the body for the prolonged trance of ritual work.

• *Lie where you are, and make your body comfortable... settle in place... and let gravity do its job... pulling you gently and evenly to the earth...*

• *Take a deep breath... and let it out... again, breathe deep, in and out... and again... now focus your attention on your feet... feel your feet... move them... wiggle your toes... now clench your feet hard... hold it... hold... and release... and clench... and release... let your feet relax, releasing all the tension...feeling the difference as the muscles relax... and let your attention withdraw from your feet... pulling back... as though they vanish into mist...*

• *Now focus your attention on your calves and ankles... feel their bones and muscles... move them a little... and now clench them hard... hold it... and release the tension... and clench... and release... relaxing your calves and ankles completely... and withdrawing your attention from them... as though the mist covered them...*

• *And focus now on your thighs and knees... flex the muscles of your thighs, keeping the rest of your legs relaxed...flex and feel the flesh... and tighten them hard... hold... and release... and clench... and relax, relax completely, withdrawing your attention... the mist covering...*

•*Your awareness focuses on your hips and loins... the muscles and complex joints, the lowest belly... flex your hips and loins... and clench... and release... tighten... and release... allow your whole lower body to relax... all tension flowing away... awareness pulling back...the mist covering all.*

• *Now turn your awareness to your hands... move your hands, feeling the bones and tendons... and clench your hands... hold... and release... tighten... and release... feeling your hands relax completely... withdrawing your awareness, as the mist covers them...*

• *Focus on your forearms and wrists... move and flex them, feeling their structure... now tighten them... hold... and relax... clench... and release, relaxing completely, withdrawing awareness, the mist rising.*

• *Bring your attention to your upper arms and elbows... flex and move them... then clench... hold... and release... and clench... and relax, feeling the tension drain from them... relaxing as your awareness is pulled back... now the mist covers your arms and legs... warm and relaxed... all tension draining away...*

• *Turn your attention to your belly and lower back... flex the muscles, and feel the complex of organs... then tighten... hold... and release... clench... and release, letting all tension flow away... letting awareness withdraw... the mist rising...*

• *As your awareness focuses on your chest and back... move and flex, keeping your body relaxed... feel your chest and back... and clench... hold... and relax... tighten... and relax... releasing tension... and withdrawing your attention...*

• *Your awareness turning now to your neck and shoulders... feeling the muscles and bones... flexing... and tighten... hold... and release... and clench... and relax your neck and shoulders, letting the mist cover your body... warm and calm... all tension released...*

• *Now your awareness turns to the back of the head, and ears... focus on them, and flex... and clench... and hold... and release... tighten... and relax, letting your awareness withdraw... the mist rising...*

11

• *And focus on your face and scalp... feel the complex of muscles and structures... move your face... then tighten... hold... and release... tight... and relax completely, withdrawing your attention from your head... the mist closing over you...*

• *And so you are at rest... your body relaxed... centered peacefully in the mist... every muscle warm and comfortable... From this relaxed place, so many things are possible... it is the door to the mind...*

• *So remember... remember this feeling... and know that by that memory you may return to this place of comfort... this peace... with ease... when you will... now rest here a moment... and remember...*

• *So you remember this state... but now you will return to your body... sure in your relaxation... able to easily return to this feeling... As you take a deep breath... let your breath flow through you... and let your awareness return to your body... warm and comfortable... Move your body... breathe deep... sit up... and remember...*

• A Fire & Water Entrancement

To prepare your mind for ritual you can try this simple technique. It is best if you have practiced rhythmic breathing before beginning this exercise, but many will find it instructive with no other training.

You will need to find a simple bowl for clear water and a candle. Arrange a comfortable seat, where your back can be straight. Arrange the bowl and candle so that you can comfortably reach them from your seat. If you prefer, turn off electric lights. When you are ready, take your seat before the water and light the candle.

Begin a pattern of rhythmic breathing, beginning with three counted breaths. Allow your body to begin to relax as you simply observe your breath. Continue to listen to your breath throughout the exercise.

With your work hand, place a drop of water on your forehead. Keeping your body relaxed, concentrate on the feel of the water on your skin. Let it fill your awareness, and allow all other awareness to fade, as you notice only the feel of the water on your skin.

Focus your gaze on the flame. Let the form and light of the fire be the concentration of your vision. Let is fill your eyes, as you see only the light of the flame.

Take three deep breaths, holding, together, the concentrations on the feeling of the water and the vision of the fire, feeling your breath flowing through you, and then say:

Between Fire & Water, I find my balance.

Observe yourself, calmly. Breathe deeply and regularly. Let your concentration always return to the simple focuses of breath, water and fire, allowing your body to relax. Remember this feeling, and know that you can find it again.

From this start, you can Widen your awareness to your altar-top or temple, always returning to your focus as you work the rite.

• Bone, Breath & Blood

• *Stand firm, and take three complete breaths. Find and release tensions in your body as you breathe.*

• *Keep your breath rhythmic, and focus on the feeling of your feet touching the ground or floor. For a moment, let your whole attention be on the place where your feet touch the world.*

• *Close your eyes, and find the pulse of your heart; in your chest, in your veins, feel the salt flow of your life.*

• *Breathe deep, and feel the air flow through you, connecting you with the whole world.*

• *Stand firm, on the land. Feel the beating of your heart, and breathe deep. Finally, imagine that a cool white light is shining from your forehead.*

• *With your attention focused on these things, open your eyes. Maintain these concentrations, and widen your awareness to the symbols and words of the rite as you begin your ritual.*

For those with little or no experience with mental magical skills, these simple exercises should be practiced regularly until they are easy and natural. The ability to sit calmly, without distraction, while focused on a simple complex of symbols or ideas for even a few minutes will begin the skills needed for the next steps. Once even a basic ability with these exercises is reached, the student should add Open meditation to the work.

13

A Word about Open Meditation

In the course of working with students I find a continuing resistance to the systematic practice of basic Open Meditation. By this term I mean the practice of concentrating attention on a single object, such as the breath, while allowing other thought and sensation to flow by the attention without attachment. This technique is preliminary to further trance and even to ritual work and should be a common part of any program of mental practice. Beginning students, however, do find reasons to balk.

Some seem to find the business of sitting motionless, pursuing nothing except mental activity, to be chafing. To this the only answer can be that any new skill has its basic methods, and most of them involve some inconvenience in early phases. Whether stretching the hands for the piano or lying face down for push-ups, discomfort is often part of learning. So we can only tell students that the results will justify the work of learning to sit motionless. Fortunately for these students a practicing Druid spends rather more time in the trances associated with ritual, than in motionless trance.

Some students mistake this practice for the attempt to 'stop thinking'. In some of the world's mystical systems this does seem to be a goal, with great value placed on finding and enhancing the silence between thoughts. Druidic lore doesn't suggest that the finding of motionless silence is, in itself, a core goal. It seems to occur spontaneously in some students, but it isn't central to the work.

Rather the point of this method for the system we're building is the development of a detached observer in the self – a point of observation for all that passes, within or without. The student learns to maintain her equanimity – engage her passions at need and to step away when she must. The work of Pagan spiritual practice can arouse the passions; can stir up ones mental contents. The ability to stand in a place of neutrality and peace offers a special strength in spiritual work, whether it's dealing with one's emotions, gazing into the Underworld, or facing the Gods.

It is common to confuse basic trance with the work of Open Meditation. They are, in fact, closely related, but there is an important distinction. Basic trance is the primary mental preparation for further trance and ritual work, induced by relaxing the body, focusing the attention and suspending critical observation (or 'attachment' as some say). We have taught this state through the Fire and Water induction, and the Bone, Breath and Blood exercise. Either of those exercises, among many other similar forms, produces the focused poise that leads to other trance states.

Open Meditation can be understood as an extension of that poise into a longer experience sustained by will. By directing the concentration upon a single focus – watching the breath being our most usual method – we locate the still point. As our thoughts and impressions flow around us, we keep returning our awareness to the focus as we sit in stillness. By sustaining the relaxation, concentration and detachment of basic trance we allow the mind and emotions to relax in turn, releasing the 'knots and kinks' of daily life.

Open meditation is an excellent accompaniment to the regular work of ritual purification. The Water and Fire clear away the spiritual cobwebs and parasites of daily spiritual life in the world. Open meditation deprives your personal inner imps and larvae of their food and weakens their grip.

So we begin the formal work of mental training by learning to abide calmly among our own thoughts and feelings. If no other good were gained from the work of Druidry, the ability to stand at peace amid the swirl of life's impulses would pay for all. In order to work the system I'm presenting here the student will have to simply choose to set to it, and develop the basic skills that support all further work. We will refer often to the 'Druid's Peace" in this work – by this we mean that steady and unmoved center. In addition to this Peace, we will learn a set of active meditations, but the Peace is the basis of them all, because the Peace grants access to the management of the mind by will.

Open meditation is as basic to mental training as aerobic exercise is to training the body. Some students will take to it readily; others may find it more difficult. Its value and results speak for themselves and to neglect it in early training is to deprive yourself of future resources.

Working Open Meditation
First Stage:
• First find your seat, in a position that can be comfortably maintained with your spine straight.
• Begin patterned breathing. Work the Blood, Breath and Bone induction.
• If you wish to work a simple shrine opening, do so now. Practice maintaining basic trance as you speak and do the ritual gestures. Return to motionless basic trance following the work.

Second Stage:
• Choose a point of focus for your concentration. Initially you should continue to use the breath.

• With your attention focused simply sit and maintain that focus. You choose not to give attention to any specific thought that arises, whether about the object of concentration or any other thing. Each time that you notice a thought or specific impression holding your attention, return your attention to the focus. That is the entire basic technique. Like raising an arm or taking a step it is the act of will that brings the attention back to the focus.

• As you practice you will begin to notice more quickly when you have drifted, and be able to hold your concentration on the focus for longer without breaks. This is the first level of success in this practice.

Closing

• Always end the session of meditation formally, with the recitation of a closing charm and/or other formal gesture.

• Contemplation Meditation

In parallel with Open Meditation we begin the next stage of training and focusing the attention and will. In Open Meditation we focus on an essentially empty symbol, such as the breath, and allow thought to flow by without attachment. In Contemplation Meditation you choose a specific pattern or symbol as the focus of your attention. In many cases the symbol – such as the Hallows or a symbol from lore, an idol or a painted symbolic image – may be physically present. It is also common to contemplate a mental construct image. You visualize, imagine or conceive the symbol in your mind, and observe it as if it were in front of you.

In this exercise the goal is similar to Open Meditation. You intend to keep the symbol always the entire focus of your attention. You may find your mind 'thinking about' the symbol – your task is to return attention directly to the object of Contemplation, without attachment to the flow of consideration about it. In this way we hope to allow the reality of the symbol to enter our awareness directly, and deeply. There is always time to think about these matters – meditation is a time set aside for other mental goals.

The technique of Contemplation is core to most of the higher-end of ritual and magical trance. As you work your way through ritual the ability to address each action with a whole and focused mind, to experience each thing for its unique power, is key to effective results. You learn to be in the presence of the Gods themselves, while maintaining the Peace and Power of your own Center. However, we can begin with much more modest goals

Three Primary Contemplations

1: Two Powers, Three Worlds, Four Quarters. You will develop the ability to easily bring the Two into your awareness, and you can then use their flow and circulation as the object of Contemplation. Set the circulation to turning in yourself, and allow your breath to keep the flow as you turn the focus of your attention to the feel and experience of the Two. Without attached consideration, allow yourself to observe the flow and shine, at peace. Each time you find yourself following a 'train of thought', simply return your attention to the continuing flow of the Two. Finish with balance and a blessing.

2: The Hallows. In this you will meditate with open eyes, focusing your attention on your fully operative Hallows of ritual. You will sit before your shrine or ritual arrangement, with the Fire lit, the Well blessed and the Tree and all cleansed with Fire and Water. You allow your gaze to fall on the whole pattern of your ritual tools and symbols, experiencing their form and meaning without attachment to any flow of thought. Finish with balance and a blessing.

3: Nature Contemplation. This practice is described in the Dedicant's work, but it should certainly be part of your regular practice. Find a place where you can observe a bit of nature, preferably with no visible thing obviously made by humans. You might choose a specific great tree, or a stream or other water, or any natural spot, but it is good to practice this also in more ordinary natural settings. You find a seat and with your Peace and Power on you allow the reality of the place to be the object of your contemplation, without attachment to idea or emotion, to beauty or ill. Finish with balance and a blessing.

• Contemplation; The Practice

The Shrine is set as usual, with an object for contemplation centrally located — a symbolic card or image, a deity, flame, or the Three Hallows themselves. This technique can be applied to music as well, though music may be more inductive to reverie than to concentration. Contemplation can also be fixed on a phrase or an envisioned image, but to begin it is best to contemplate a material object.

1: Basic Trance: The Blood, Breath and Bone Exercise:

• *Stand or be seated firmly, spine erect, arms able to relax.*

• *Take three Complete Breaths and continue to breathe.*

• *Become aware of your body, where you are supported on the ground by your firm bones. Be aware of your bones, holding you upright as you feel your flesh relax.*

• *Continue to breathe fully, and focus attention on the sound of the breath. Concentrate inward, listening only to the sound of your breath.*

• *Turn your attention inward, and hear and feel the beating of blood in your veins. Feel the subtle pulse, as your breath flows and your bones uphold you.*

• *Continue this pattern as you open your eyes. Allow yourself to remain relaxed, focusing only on your Blood, Breath and Bone.*

• *Recite this charm:*

Bone uphold me
Breath inspire me

Blood sustain me
In this holy work.

• *Return to silent breathing and listening within.*

• *From this state there are two basic kinds of meditation with which to begin your work. You can proceed to open meditation, or choose an object of contemplation. Ritual actions can also be performed, while maintaining Basic Trance state. We continue to contemplation:*

2: Meditation

• *Continue your basic trance, settling peacefully into blood, breath and bone.*

• *Open your eyes, and bring your gaze gently upon the object of your contemplation.*

• *Allow your gaze to focus on the object of contemplation, and only on that object, concentrating your attention to that single object or symbol or sequence of ideas. Just as in Open Meditation you focused on your breath, allowing all thought to flow by ungrasped, so in Contemplation Meditation you focus your attention on a powerful symbol, and allow only considerations and perceptions of that symbol to fill your mind.*

• *First always return to the material form of the object, its real presence. From there you may carefully open to ideas concerning the object. This will inevitably lead to associated thought. Whenever that happens, simply return your awareness to the visible (or audible) form of the object.*

• *The goal is to extend the periods in which your awareness is wholly occupied by a single object, especially one with spiritual or symbolic meaning.*

• *When the time is sufficient, close your eyes, return to basic trance, then close.*

3: Closing

• *Always end the session of meditation formally, with the recitation of a closing charm and / or other formal gesture.*

The blessings of the Holy Ones be on me and mine
My blessings on all beings, with peace on thee and thine
The Fire, the Well, the Sacred Tree
Flow and Flame and Grow in me
Thus do I remember the work of the Wise.

Contemplation of the Land

It is vital for you to make a true and deep contact with the forms and processes of nature. One way to approach that is to use basic trance to open your self to those patterns. While it is good to actually leave the city when possible, it is not necessary to go deep into the wild to do this work. Every city has park land, back yards, even decorative trees that allow contact with forms not shaped by humankind.

When you have a little skill in finding your Peace and Power, go out to a place where you can sit quietly on the grass or a low bench or mat. If you can find a place where more than one kind of natural form occurs - trees, herbs, beasts, stones, streams - then that is best. Seat yourself as comfortably as possible and begin your pattern of rhythmic breathing.

Sitting with your eyes closed, find the rhythm of your breath, and work one of the basic mental exercises. After a while allow yourself to begin to listen to the sounds around you. Let those sounds enter your mind and flow through you, hearing all but holding to nothing. The goal is to keep your mental balance and calm no matter the input. When you wish, open your eyes. Let the sights of the natural world move through your mind. Allow your eye to flow over the forms of the natural world, even linger to look closely. But when any thought or image grasps or holds the attention, return to counting the breath and let eye and mind move on. The goal is to sit in silence, your mind transparent to the reality of the woodland, offering no obstacle to the flow of nature's sights and sounds.

The final phase of this work is to stand and walk while maintaining the "open eye." When this can be managed with a minimal number of breaks, you will have a skill that can help you in every part of your life from labor's drudgery to the sublime moments of vision and magic.

If you wish, your efforts to become aware of the Spirits in any specific place can be expressed in a spoken charm or prayer. When you have felt welcomed in any natural place it is always good to give a small offering, perhaps spilling a little drink upon the ground, and saying:

The world is in me, and I am in the world
The Spirit in me is the Spirit in the world.
To you, place of beauty, place of honor,
To you (name and describe place)
I bring this offering in peace.
From the Deep in me to the Deep in you
From my Fire to your Fire
A gift of honor, a gift of worship
In hope of your welcome
That there be peace between us
In all things
Be it so!

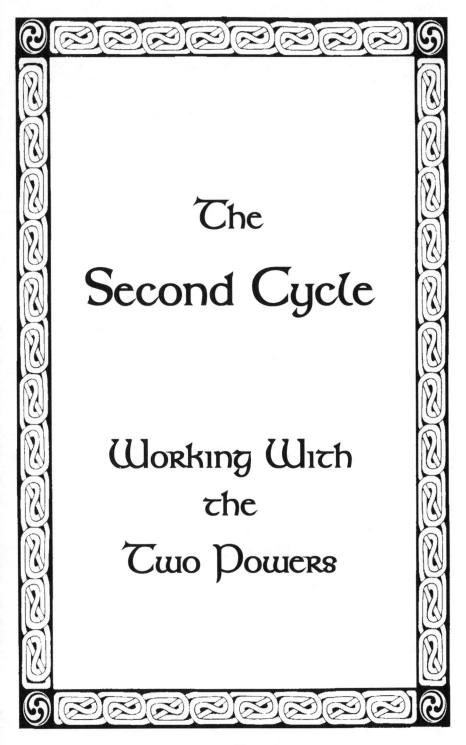

The
Second Cycle

Working With
the
Two Powers

The Second Cycle: Underworld & Heaven

The work of traditional magic is not quietist. The ancient wise did not teach that the highest wisdom came by simply sitting in silence, waiting for a voice. They did not teach that all wisdom lay within the individual, or that only turning within could lead to good results. Rather, ancient wisdom teaches that divine power lies in everything, both within the personal soul and outside it, both deep in the Self and in nature around us.

So, to seek wisdom and power is to seek to know both internal and external reality. With Open Meditation we began by working with the contents and habits of the untrained mind. We learn to calm our hearts and to lift our perspective above the cloudy drift of our common thought and impulse. This is, in essence an act of will, and it begins the training of the will, which is fundamental to all spiritual and magical practice. The remainder of the work of trance and vision depends on the ability to turn the mind away from distraction and focus on an internal experience at will.

The work of the Two Powers begins the process of connecting the internal self with an external spiritual reality. It is a method of 'Grounding & Centering'. This term is seldom used with precision. I use 'grounding' to refer to making a connection between the internal human patterns and a source of power or potential outside of the self. The term arose from the work of disposing of excess energy following a rite - 'grounding' it like electricity into the earth. It has become combined with Yogic ideas, and worked into a Pagan context in many ways. I use 'centering' to refer to the willed control of the flow and pattern of the energy brought into the self. Often this is arranged in a set of internal 'centers'. In the next Cycle we will introduce a more detailed vision of the Center. For now the flow of the Two Powers in the central channel of the body makes the point. So in grounding and centering we own ourselves to the pre-existing flow of two primal, impersonal spiritual powers, and we make a whole and holy pattern of those powers in ourselves, by the power of vision and will.

From a traditionalist perspective, it is difficult to demonstrate that this sort of 'energy work' was practiced by Celts or other European sorcerers. Indic systems appear to have worked with impersonal forces from early times, though the kind of work presented here is certainly a modern invention. However, from the perspective of spirit-arte, the vision of the magician standing in the cosmic center, flowing and burning with the primal powers of the cosmos and wielding them in her hands is a fine Pagan version of being prepared in personal power for dealings with arch-beings.

Finally, these methods are intrinsically healing and restorative. To order your internal patterns and empower them with greater powers builds strength both of soul and of body. While that healing isn't a primary purpose of this work, I can recommend the practices based on that alone.

Energy Work with the Two Powers

The Two Powers: Underworld and Heavens

The Underworld Power: The primary image that evokes the underworld power is of the waters that seep, pool and flow beneath the surface on which we dwell. These waters are in some way connected with all the world's waters, an ever-flowing current. In that water is dissolved every nutrient required to sustain all life, nutrients derived from the natural processes of decay and dissolution. From this matrix every being arises, all the bounty of the world. Even crystal condenses from the waters under the Earth.

In Celtic lore this primal water can be connected with the primal Mother - Danu, Mother of the gods and goddesses. She can be envisioned as the ocean of undifferentiated awareness, her mind the ever-flowing current of being deep beneath our surface life. Every individual manifestation is rooted and connected through the waters of the "all-mind."

When we contact the underworld power we reach deep into the dark, to the current from the past, to the flow and store of the memory of the worlds, the undifferentiated flow of possibility that is sometimes called the "chaos of potential." Through our underworld awareness we can reach out to touch the roots of other minds, other forms of consciousness. We grasp the raw material, that can be shaped by magic into new forms and manifestations.

The Heaven Power: The primary image that evokes the heaven power is the light of sun and moon, the great lights that wheel and turn in their eternal order. When this power falls upon the earth it draws forth individual lives, stirring and transforming the potentials of the waters, providing the pattern that allows individual existences to grow. In the same way, this heaven power is made real to us in fire. Just as the sun warms the waters of the earth, so the sacred fire warms the contents of the magic cauldron, transforming raw materials into food, medicine or sorcery.

In Celtic lore this primal fire can be connected with the first Father - Bel, the ancestor of the gods and goddesses. He can be understood as the spark of kindling, the point around which individual beings grow from the matrix of potential. He inspires the creative power that allows us to shape reality from the river of fate.

When we contact the heaven power we feel the inner light, the precipitating, crystallizing force that makes us who we are. We grasp the organizing pattern of cosmos, that allows continuity of form and life, which

25

can be called the world order. Through heavenly awareness we gain the power of shaping, that orders the flow of potential, that allows us to bind fate to some small degree, according to our will.

These two powers are the dynamic tension that produces our apparent reality. They are present in every being, every spirit. In humankind they flow in our bodies and souls, and can be directed to some extent by will and imagination, or by emotion and its accompanying impulses. So the student learns to become aware of the two powers as they flow in the worlds and in herself. She learns to use will and vision to accumulate the powers in body and soul, and to draw strength from them. From this skill many kinds of practical magic arise, beginning with the power of the gate, the place at the boundary between heaven and the underworld.

Visualization and Energy Work

Once you have mastered the basic trance - that is, once you can sit quietly, with both body and mind relaxed but alert - you can move on to the work of visualization and energy. Both visualization and energy work require the ability to produce mental experiences that seem to be sensory, to the mind. In energy work we use imagination to produce the feeling of energy flowing through the body, and in visualization we use it to produce mental images. Of course all the other senses are also employed in producing a fully-realized vision - inner hearing, touch, etc. play their part.

The Two Powers script given here is an example of using vision skills to produce the feeling of energy flow in the body. We build the feel of the cool earth-power, the warm light, the tingle or thrill of the flow, the vision of the fire flowing in us. Such a script should really be experienced as a guided exercise, at first. This often happens in our public rituals, but solitary students may need to resort to recording the script in their own voice, at a stately, gentle pace.

The Two Powers – Full Scripted Induction

This is a basic meditation intended to link the Druid's spirit and flesh to the currents of Earth and Sky. It is based on methods that have become known in Pagan work as 'grounding and centering'. All these methods are meant to connect the student to spiritual powers in the cosmos, and to provide balanced channels of flow for those powers in the personal soul. Some form of this technique should precede almost any work of worship or magic. The Two Powers model is based on core concepts in Indo-European lore, but is not, by any means, the only vision or mythic model useful in our Druidry.

The work begins by seating yourself, or standing, in a comfortable position at your meditation seat. Here follows a script for a version of the Two Powers work. You should read through the script until you are familiar with its pattern, or perhaps even read it onto a tape for the first several exercises. Soon, with practice, you will know the basic order, and be able to proceed from memory. The best practice is to memorize the sequence of images, but this is made much easier by a few repetitions with spoken guidance.

The Script

• *Begin, O seeker of wisdom, with your breath... breathe deeply, from your belly... in... and out... make your body comfortable... stretch if you need to, settle in place... and focus on your breath... observe your breath as it flows in and out of your body... and with each breath, allow your body to relax... let your breath carry away tension from your flesh.. relaxing your feet and legs... letting your belly soften and relax... breathing away tension from your shoulders and arms... from your neck... relaxing your face and mouth, your eyes... with each breath your body becoming warmer, comfortable and relaxed... your mind alert and prepared for magic...*

• *Now, with your body still and calm, imagine that from your feet, or the base of your spine, roots begin to grow downward... roots reaching and growing into the earth, down through soil and stone... deepening and spreading... reaching to touch the waters under the Earth... the Earth current... the dark, cool, magnetic power that nourishes and sustains life... as your roots touch this current it is drawn in and up toward your body... your breath draws the Earth power upward... into your body... the invisible, magnetic power fills your legs, energizing and strengthening... waters rise from the earth, into your legs... rising... into your loins...*

27

and pooling in your loins, a cauldron of Earth power...You breathe the power upward... rising from the earth, through your loins, rising up your spine... into your heart... pooling and filling a cauldron in your heart with healing, restoring energy... power rising from the deep, through your loins, through your heart... rising up your spine and into your head... filling a cauldron of wisdom and vision behind your eyes... and rising still, filling all your body and flowing out again through the crown of your head... through your hands... flowing out around your body and back into the earth... the power under the Earth flows in you... grounding you in the source of life...

• Now imagine the sky overhead... The sun and moon and, far beyond them, the stars... imagine a single star at the center of the sky, shining directly over your head... the center of your inner sky, your own pole-star...see a flash of light shining down from that star... streaming down between moon and sun... gold, silver and blue-white light... the bright, warm, electric power of the sky... the light touches your head, filling and illuminating the cauldron like sun on still water... shining from above... filling your head with warm, awakening power...flowing down into your heart... warming the cauldron... shining down through head and heart, illumining the waters... downward to reach your loins... The cauldron shines with sky power in your loins... Tingling, electrical light in head, heart and loins... the light flows downward into Earth, and you are shining and flowing with the mingled powers of Earth and sky... the raw material of magic... the chaos of potential and the world order...

• These powers are balanced in you... yours to shape and use... always with you in some degree... But for now, allow the powers to recede... waters to the Earth, light to the sky... knowing that each time you attune to them you become more attuned, more at one with the powers... breath deep... and allow your awareness to return to your common senses... as you open your eyes...

Basic Two Powers Awareness

This is a basic meditation intended to link the Druid's spirit and flesh to the currents of Earth and Sky. It is based on methods that have become known in Pagan work as 'grounding and centering'. All these methods are meant to connect the student to spiritual powers in the cosmos, and to encourage balance in the personal soul. Some form of this technique should precede almost any work of worship or magic.

• Find your seat or your stance, and relax into a basic trance.
• Envision dark, rich power that flows like water under your feet. Take three deep, complete breaths and imagine that Underworld Water flowing up into your body
• Envision bright, inspiring power that shines like Fire above your head. Take three deep, complete breaths and imagine that Power of the Heavens shining down into your body.
• Take three deep breaths and envision the Light and the Dark, mingling in your blood, in your breath, in your heart.
• Proceed to your work.

A Primary Circulation of the Two Powers

1: Find your Peace and bring the Two Powers into balance into yourself.

2: Focus on the Waters, and bring them into a current flowing upward through your legs to meet in your loins, then travel up through the center of your body on a line with your spine. In later exercises we will add the Three Cauldrons, but for now focus on a s single clear channel, that reaches all the way to the head, that fills and overflows into the whole body, creating a circulation of the Earth Power as your breath continues to draw and drive the Power from beneath.

3: Focus on the Light, and open your head to the shining pattern of Fire as it shines down onto and into you, and see it shining in a clear channel that fills the head, shines down the center into the loins and fills the body with glowing warmth and pattern.

4: The Water becomes filled with the Fire. With your breath you move them through you, and the flow of the Two becomes Light and Shadow, Fire and Water together, circulating through the body, connecting you with the Deep and with the Height.

5: Hold you palms up, and fill your hands with the flow of the Two. From this stance many works can be done. Contemplation of this state, as described in the First Cycle, is always profitable.

6: To end, allow the force of the flow to recede as you release your breath, and the power to flow back to center from your hands. Conclude with a final act or charm.

Experiencing the Two Powers

• Learning to smoothly balance the Powers is the first step in really working with them. It is also a good idea to spend some time learning to focus upon and feel the presence of each of the Two Powers individually.

•Find your Peace, and bring the Two Powers in balance into yourself.

• Begin with the Underworld power. Focus your awareness on the Deep Power, and let it flow fully into your awareness. Using your breath, draw more and more of the Waters into yourself, focus your contemplation upon the Waters, and upon your connection with the Underworld.

• Firmly return to a fully balanced state of the Two.

• Focus your awareness on the Heaven power. Feel the shining of the Light of the Sky and let it flow fully into your awareness. Using your breath draw more and more of the Fire into yourself, focus your contemplation upon the Fire and upon your connection with the Heavens.

• Firmly return to a fully balanced state of the Two. Circulate the Powers in yourself, and end the exercise with the Blessing.

The Caher Draoi Exercise

• *Seat yourself for working, and work the Blood, Breath and Bone entrancement:*

• *Stand or be seated firmly, spine erect, arms able to relax.*

• *Take three Complete Breaths and continue to breathe.*

• *Become aware of your body, where you are supported on the ground by your firm bones. Be aware of your bones, holding you upright as you feel your flesh relax.*

• *Continue to breathe fully, and focus attention on the sound of the breath. Concentrate inward, listening only to the sound of your breath.*

• *Turn your attention inward, and hear and feel the beating of blood in your veins. Feel the subtle pulse, as your breath flows and your bones uphold you.*

• *Continue this pattern as you open your eyes. Allow yourself to remain relaxed, focusing only on your Blood, Breath and Bone.*

• *Recite this charm:*

Bone uphold me
Breath inspire me
Blood sustain me
In this holy work.

• *Draw the Two Powers into you, in a primary circulation:*

• *Focus on the Underworld Waters, and bring them into a current flowing upward through your legs to meet in your loins . . . then travel up through the center of your body . . . on a line with your spine. Focus on a single clear channel . . . that reaches all the way to the head . . . that fills and overflows into the whole body . . . creating a circulation of the Earth Power as your breath continues to draw and drive the Power from beneath.*

• *Focus on the Light of the Heavens . . . and open your head to the shining pattern of Fire . . . as it radiates down onto and into you . . . and see it shining in a clear channel . . . that fills the head . . . shines down the center into the loins . . . and fills the body with glowing warmth and whirling pattern.*

• *The Water becomes filled with the Fire . . . With your breath you move them through you . . . and the flow of the Two becomes Light and Shadow . . . Fire and Water together . . . one thing made of two . . . a deep, shining essence . . . circulating through the body, connecting you with the Deep and with the Height.*

31

• *Hold your hands before you... cupped as though to hold water. Breathe deep, and let your breath draw and drive the Essence of the Two... each breath increasing and intensifying the Two in your hands. Let the Waters fill your hands... and flow over the fingers... and the Fire kindle as a flame atop the Waters... moving the Waters with its heat. Let the Fire grow so bright that your hands shine... incandescent... making a sphere of light and flame around your hands. The Waters flow into this Flame... feed it... and are turned into mist, that flows from the surface of the sphere. Move your hands until you get a feel for how you can manifest and hold this spherical form of the Two.*

• *Bring your hands to your heart... and place the sphere of the Two into yourself, letting it flow and shine in your center... breathe deep, and envision the sphere of Fire and Water growing, larger and larger, until it encompasses your whole body... a single Sphere surrounding your whole self. Conceive the Fire as shining downward from above... through the self, then flaming up around the Sphere. Conceive the Water as rising up from below... then fountaining down around the Sphere. Intensify this dual current as you can and will. Let your breath bring the power... and return to that incandescent fire and spreading mist.*

• *It is the Waters that bring the all-potential to the Mage's work... It is the Fire that brings the power to manifest specific goals... At the edge of the Sphere of the Two Powers the Fire brings shape from the Deep... From this formula many works proceed.*

• *This Sphere is the Caher Draoi, the Druid's Fortress... the inner sanctum, the invisible chapel of the magician's power. In it you may set any sign, will any shape... and from it many works of magic can be done...*

• *Set the sign of the Gate at your heart, the Well in your loins, the Fire in your head... Conceive the Dual Flow through your body to be as the root and branch of the World Tree... This is the first manifestation of the Nemeton of Vision.. the Otherworld reality of the ritual space in which magic is made... Into this Fortress we call what we will.. and send forth what we will in turn.*

• *Now rest a while in contemplation of the Caher Draoi...*

• *When you are done, refocus on the flow of energies in the sphere...*
By will and vision, see the sphere shrink... smaller and smaller until it
encloses your heart... and allow that vision to fade... returning to Bone,
Breath and Blood...
• *Close with a prayer if you wish:*

The Blessings of the Holy Ones be on me and mine
My Blessings on all beings,
With peace on three and thine
The Fire, the Well, the Sacred Tree
Flow and Flame and Grow in me
Thus do I remember the work of the wise

Works of the Two Powers:
1: Purification

The ability to gather and direct the Earth and Sky Powers is often seen as the operative power behind or within a number of simple rituals. One of the most common of those is purification or cleansing of tools, or of homes, beds, etc. Here I will present the simple ritual form, and then describe the details of focusing and directing the Two Powers to empower that rite.

A Simple Charm of Purification

The object is brought to the shrine, or into the circle. The Water and Fire is present, and hallowed as you will, perhaps using this simple charm:

The Fire, the Well, the Sacred Tree
Flow and Flame and grow in me.
In Land, Sea and Sky,
Below and on high,
Let the Water be blessed and the Fire be hallowed.

Sprinkle the object with water from the Tobar. Cause the Deep Power to flow over and through it as you say three times:

By the holy Power of the Deep
The Waters of the Dark, the secret Well,
Be free of every ill or every bane
Washed clean by magic's might, as I do will.

If you can, light an open flame from your Tintean. Make a large offering of incense, hold the object in the smoke, and fill it with the light of the Sky, as you say:

By the shining Power of the Sky
The Fire of Sorcery, the Heaven's Light
Let every ill or bane now flee away,
By my word and will, and magic's might.

Speak a Briocht proper to the work, or use a version of this general charm:

By the Might of the Waters and the Light of the Fire
Let all ill turn away from this (object), and all good flow
to it.
Let no ill approach by Land or Sea or Sky
Let no ill approach by Day or by Night
Nor in the Spaces Between
By the Might of the Waters and the Light of the Fire
Let all ill turn away!

Draw and invoking Triskelion over the object, saying:

By Fire, Well, and Tree
By Land, sky and Sea
By Gods, Dead, and Sidhe
By my word and by my will,
Bíodh se amhlaidh!

It is best to immediately use the object for its intended purpose, and then put it in its place on the shrine.

The Inner Work:

1: Enter Basic Trance using the Fire & Water or Bone, Breath and Blood exercise.

2: Work the Caher Draoi, and produce the Triessence in the heart.

3: Re-separate the Triessence into the Two Powers, Water in the left hand and Fire in the right for most people.

4: Charge the Hallows with the Two Powers as you recite the charm. See the Water charging the Well, the Light charging the Fire, and the Triessence reforming in the Tree, with each reflected in the other. Conceive the Caher to encompass both yourself and the Hallows.

5: Maintaining the separation in the hands, take up the Well. Holding it in the left hand, direct the Underworld Power by breath and will to charge the Cauldron ever more strongly. Continue that for some while, until you can feel a strong charge in the tool and the water of the Well. Sprinkle the target with the water, while reciting the charm.

6: As you sprinkle and chant, allow powerful images of water to direct the Underworld flow. See waves of it wash through the target, dissolving all ill, or even dissolving the target itself if you are banishing a spirit or a force. See the Waters carrying the mess away into the deep. Continue to direct the power through you, and through the sprinkled water, through the target and into the earth as the charm is repeated three times.

7: Replace the Well on the Shrine, and take up Fire from the Altar Fire. Draw the Heaven Fire into your right hand, and charge the flame or smoke strongly with the power, using breath and will. You may simply lift the fire-bowl itself, or you might take fire by lighting several sticks of good incense and allowing them to burn with open flame for a moment, before blowing them out and continuing to charge with the smoke as the charm is repeated three times.

8: As you shine the light or spread the smoke over the target, allow images of light, warmth and fire to fill the object. See the Fire burn away all that is imperfect or ill in the target, driving ill away completely. The Fire also fills the form of an object to be purified, filling it with positive blessing, following the emptying cleansing of the Water. See the target shine with the Light of the heavens.

9: Replacing the Fire on the Shrine, hold the object to be purified in your hands, or beneath your hands. Renew the Caher Draoi, producing the Triessence strongly, and seeing it formed from the Fire and Water in the target as well. Expand the sphere of the Caher Draoi to contain the target, and bring the Two into whole and perfect balance, declaring the target to be cleansed by reciting the purification charm three times. Draw the triskel over the target to seal the pattern, reciting the final charm just once.

This charm can also be used with no physical symbols at all, using only the envisioned Fire and Water. Tradition teaches that the work is best done by including material symbols, but with some skill the work can be done effectively without them. Students are advised to learn the technique using physical water and fire, whenever possible.

2: Warding

The use of the Two Powers for warding is based on the shaping of the Triessence through will and vision. It can be accompanied by a spoken charm or some physical gesture, but can always be done silently. The skilled Druid will develop patterns that can be erected nearly instantly, at need.

Choosing a warding vision is a matter of finding symbols that both excite the heart and produce the feeling of centered strength. Many people find visions of ancient or traditional weapons useful. The Spear of Lugh is a powerful protection, which can be combined with the starry Cloak of Brigid as a warding charm. Of course such a charm works best for those who keep the rites of both Brigid and Lugh.

The Powers can also be used more directly, the Underworld Power to dissolve and ground away any attack, and the Heaven Power to actively drive away by light and fire. This leads directly back into the Caher Draoi which is itself a powerful protection when made intense and sharp.

An equally powerful approach to warding is the Convoking of Cosmos, in which the cosmic diagram is manifested in vision within your personal sphere. By standing firm in the Sacred Center no ill can reach you. That vision is taught in the Third Cycle of this book's work.

Here are two charms for warding. I provide the Irish text for those who prefer it. The English will be sufficient for most english-speakers.

•The Cloak and Spear

Stand facing east, if possible, and clasp hands at the heart. Raise the Caher Draoi as you say:

Powers of the Earth and Sky
Rooted deep and crowned high.

Cumhachtaí an domhain agus an spear
Fréamhaithe íseal agus choróin ard.

Open hands out, as the Cloak of Brigid is envisioned covering the Caher, Say:
Cloak of the High One, cover us.
Peace upon us
Ease upon us
Protection upon us
By the power of the Starry Deep.

Brat na hArdaon, clúdach linn.
Síochána orainn
Éasca orainn
Cosaint orainn
De réir an cumhacht ag an réalta sa domhain.

Point finger (or wand) to the four directions in turn, beginning in the east, saying:
Spear of the Victory eastward now stand
Turn aside ill in the name of Long-Hand
Spear of the Victory southward now stand
Turn aside ill in the name of Long-Hand
Spear of the Victory westward now stand
Turn aside ill in the name of Long-Hand
Spear of the Victory northward now stand
Turn aside ill in the name of Long-Hand

Sleá an bua soir anois seasamh
Cas ar leataobh tinn in ainm an lámh fhada

Sleá an bua seasamh dheas anois
Sleá an bua anois seasamh siar
Sleá an bua ó thuaidh anois seasamh

Hold hands out in triumph, then return to hands clasped at the heart, saying:
By Lugh the Mighty and Brigid the High
Thus I am guarded in Land, Sea and Sky.
Trí Lugh láidir agus Bríd ard
ar thalamh ar muir agus sa spéir mé slán

The Inner Work

1: Enter Basic Trance
2: Raise the Caher Draoi, and widen the sphere to include the area to be warded.
3: Envision the Cloak of Brigid, deep blue and starry, hemmed in green, settling over the sphere, and reflected below. Draw up the Deep Power and shape it into the form of the Cloak. Let that be accompanied by a nourishing

flow of love, protection and safety.

4: Bring the Fire into your hand and shape the form of the Spear of Lugh before you in the east. See it flying, unmoving, flaming at the edge of the sphere, and then turn and establish it again in the next quarter. Feel the Fire bring the light of courage and strength.

5: Hold the whole vision, of the surrounding Cloak of Starry Deep and Green Wall, and the Spear standing flaming in all directions. Feel the presence of Brigid and Lugh, as you know them, and confirm the whole work by the final charm. Allow the vision to fade to the background as you continue your work.

• Boiling the Cauldron

In this working the Caher Draoi is empowered as a spherical shield made of the Fire and Water. The Underworld Power is poured into a thick layer, and the heaven Power is placed 'beneath' it, inside the sphere. In this way the Waters are brought to boil, making a powerful shield.

Establish the Caher Draoi, saying:

Powers of the Earth & Sky,
Rooted deep and crowned high.
Rise from the deep oh ancient might.
Burn in my heart now, primal light.

Say three times, as you establish the moat:

Flow around me, shadow deep
All ill from me now to keep.

Say three times as you kindle the fire:

Heaven's flame now burn within
Let the boiling now begin.

Say three times as the Waters boil and the Fire Burns:

Fire and Shadow, boil and burn
Let the wheel of magic turn
Nothing passes that brings ill
By my word and by my will.

Inner Work

1: Raise the Caher Draoi. Establish the Triessence as a sphere surrounding the area that is to be warded.

2: Begin to draw up the Underworld Power more strongly, and with it bring images of dissolution, decay and entanglement. Shape this Shadow-power into a layer on the outward side of your sphere, surrounding you as though by a swampy moat. Conceive of this barrier as a trap for all who might do you harm.

3: Draw down the Fire of the Heavens, and concentrate it in your heart. With breath, vision and will accumulate the Light, seeing it fill the space within the sphere of Underworld Power. It becomes a second layer, made of the Heavens' Fire, burning beneath the Waters.

4: Envision the heat of the Sky Power bringing the Underworld Water to a boil, dissolving all that might enter it. This is the warding, that the dissolving power of the Waters be amplified and made even more impassable by the heat and action of the Fire, so that all that attempts to pass it be destroyed, dissolved and returned to the elements from which it arises.

Wand & Cauldron Work – A Will-Working

The Wand is held in the right hand, and the Cauldron in the left. If needed, the Wand and Cauldron can both be held in the left hand, the wand resting crosswise while the fingers hold the Cauldron. The Cauldron is generally held in the palm of the cupped hand. The Wand is gripped at its balance point, held upright, the 'scepter' end up and the 'pointing end' down. (Scepter end is the wider end, pointing end the more narrow.)

• **Throne Position:** Seated cross-legged, Cauldron at rest in left hand on thigh, Wand at rest held up as scepter on right side.

• *Five Conjuring Positions:*

- **Fadaigh - Kindling:** Cauldron held at the belly or loins, Wand held at the heart, pointing end down toward Cauldron.

- **Teasa - Heating:** The Wand's pointing end is held beneath the Cauldron, parallel to the floor

- **Mheascadh - Stirring:** The Wand's pointing end is circled around the Cauldron, whether around the mouth or all around the body, as is preferred.

- **Tarraingim - Drawing Out:** The scepter end is held across the Cauldron, then raised to draw forth the Blessing.

- **Beannacht - Blessing:** Cauldron returns to rest, Wand held out before body, or touched to forehead.

The Working:

• *Begin in throne position. Bring the Two powers into yourself, saying*

Powers of the Earth and sky,
Rooted deep and crowned high
(cumhachtaí ar domhan agus speir
fréamhaithe go domhain agus faoi choroin ard)

• *Kindling position:*

Let the Fire be kindled, let there be light in the darkness
(lig an lasair a adaim,
in iúl go mbeadh solas sa dorchadas)

• *Heating Position:*

Let the Fire come into the Water,
I set this Cauldron to boil

41

(Lig an Dóiteáin thagann isteach ar an Uisce,
leag mé an choire a fhiuchadh)
Into this Cauldron I place these Powers
That they may be boiled in the Water and the Fire
(Isteach sa choire áit mé na cumhachtaí seo
Féadfar iad a bruite ar an uisce agus an tine)
Recite or envision the elements that you would add to the spell, see them mixing into
the combining flow and flame of the Cauldron.

• *Stirring:*
Make the motion, while reciting this charm at least nine times:
Turn, Turn, Turn again
Turn, Turn, Turn again
Turn, Turn, Turn again
Let my will be done.
Cas, cas, cas arís
Cas, cas, cas arís
Cas, cas, cas arís
lig beidh mo amhlaidh

• *Drawing Forth:*
Now let the Blessing come forth
By the power of the Wand and Cauldron
By the Deep and by the Height
I bring forth the magic
(Anois, lig an bheannacht teacht amach
De réir an cumhacht ag an slat agus choire
De réir an domhain agus ag an aired
thabhairt mé amach an draíocht)

• *Blessing:*
Now let the power be in me
And the magic be mine
In my flesh and bone
In my heart and mind
And let my will be done

(thabhairt mé amach an draíocht
Agus lig an draíocht a chur ar mo
I mo chorp agus cnámh
I mo chroí agus aigne
Agus lig beidh mo a dhéanamh.)

Return to throne position, and say:
The Fire, the Well, the Sacred Tree
Flow and flame and grow in me.
The work is finished
Let it be so!
(An Dóiteáin, an Tobar, an Crann Naofa
Sreabhadh agus lasair agus fás i mo
Tá an obair críochnaithe
Lig sé a bheith mar sin!)

Healing with the Two Powers

1: A Two-Powers Healing Charm

• *The Druid stands or sits with the patient, the patient seated or lying. If the Druid has his Wand and Cauldron, then the Cauldron might sit in the lap of the patient, or be held in her hands, with a moderate amount of a healing drink in the vessel. The Druid holds the Wand. Without the Wand and Cauldron, there should still be a vessel of drink, and the raised hand of the Druid shall serve.*

• *The Druid brings the Two Powers strongly into the self, perhaps finishing with the Kindling Charm.*

• *The Druid raises her hand, or the wand, and divides the Two Powers, allowing the Dark to fill the earth beneath the patient, and the Light to accumulate in the Wand or hand. Using the breath, the Two Powers are built up, with the patient in the field between them.*

• *The Druid focuses the Light, with Wand or hand, into the drink in the Cauldron or vessel, allowing it to be charged by the images of the charm, spoken or sung three times:*

Powers of Land and Sky attend me.
Attend me powers of Earth and Sun.
Mighty Spear of Lugh defend the
Earth from which all life's begun.
Hie to me healing from the deeps
Ancient of Ancients wholeness keeps
Boon of the bright sky, healing is
Light on the lurker, illness flees
Sun gives life to Earth's broad field
Bring me Healing, Spear and Shield!

• *As the third recitation is completed the Druid focuses the Light and Shadow into the drink in the vessel, drawing the sigil over the vessel with hand or Wand. The patient then drinks the drink.*

2: A Sacrifice for Healing
The Text of the Rite:

1: Hallow the Grove.

2: Open the Gate.

3: Make the Offerings to the Three Kindreds, saying:

Now to my Sacred Fire I call
      the Threefold Kindreds, spirits all
All my allies among the Dead; Mighty and Beloved Ones,
      stand strong with me in my work,
And receive this offering. *(make the offering)*
All my allies among the Sidhe,
Red blood, green sap or Spirit Folk,
      join me on my work's journey,
And receive this offering. *(make the offering)*
All my allies among the Gods; Wisest and Mightiest Ones,
      I pray that your power burn and flow in me
So, receive this offering. *(make the offering)*

Hold up the object to be hallowed and display it to the four airts. Say:

Hear me, my kin, my allies, my elders, I pray, and make your wisdom open to me, your love flow with mine, your power strong in me, that I may do the work of the Wise. Be beside me, Mighty, Noble and Shining Ones, and give your blessing to this work of healing, that it may be blessing of restoration and wholeness for me, for I am *(your name and lineage)*, your true worshipper!
In the Mother's Love be welcome.
In the Joys of Life be welcome.
In this Sacred Grove be welcome.
And accept my sacrifices!

3: Invocation of the Healing Gods
Now I call to you Tuatha De Danann who are healers.
First to the High One, Brigid of the Fire and Water,

Daughter of the Dagda, Lady of the Mercies. Let your power be my blessing in this work of healing, and accept this offering!

And to Diancecht of the Wisdoms, who made the Silver Hand, who made the Well of Restorations, restore me, I pray by this rite, and accept this offering!

To Miach and Airmid, Children of the God of Hazels, you who turn keep the healer's ways, let your skill guide this work of the Druid's arte, and accept my offering!

4: Final Sacrifice

Let the Druid pause for a time in contemplation of these Gods, and of the Kindreds. When she is ready she prepares a final offering and says:

Hear me now, I pray, Wise and Shining Ones, Mighty Gods and Goddesses of the Curing Art. I come seeking a healing, that my flesh be made whole, and my heart be made whole, and my mind be made whole; that illness not lay my body low, that sorrow not weaken my heart, that falsehood not cloud my mind. So let my voice rise on the Fire, let my voice ring in the Well, let my call pass the Gate to the Land of Spirits. Holy Ones, accept my sacrifice!

5: Omen

An omen is taken, asking whether the Gods favor the intention of the rite. If the omen is good, the rite proceeds:

6: The Blessing of Healing

The Druid renews his center, and brings the Two Powers strongly into his Caher Draoi, producing the Triessence. He says:

Come I to the Fire and Well
A spell to weave by word and hand
I stand in power, by the Three
By Sea and Sky and by the Land
Let your power be with me in this work
And let this be a work of Blessing,

Of healing of flesh, and heart, and mind.

Take up the Blessing Cauldron, filled with pure water, and hold it in your left hand. Breathe deep and accumulate the Underworld Power into the vessel. Envision the waters growing deep and bright and thick with the cleansing power of the Deep. Take up the three charm stones, and drop them into the Cauldron as you incant three times:

Cleanse and bless, strength of the deep
Flow in this bowl of blessing
Heal and cleanse, whole and well
Blessed by Carnelian

Drop the carnelian into the Cauldron

Cleanse and bless, strength of the deep
Flow in this bowl of blessing
Heal and cleanse, whole and well
Blessed by the Amethyst

Drop the amethyst into the Cauldron

Cleanse and bless, strength of the deep
Flow in this bowl of blessing
Heal and cleanse, whole and well
Blessed by the Crystal bright

Drop the crystal into the Cauldron

Now the Druid should bathe in the waters, perhaps using a ladle or spoon to dip and pour the waters over the crown of the Head, the hands, and certainly over and part of the self that is in need of special healing. In this process the Earth Power is seen as washing away any and all ill, rinsing it down through and out of the self. Use the towel and make sure that you are well-washed in the Waters of Blessing. As the cleansing is done, incant as many times as needed:

Cleanse my flesh, heal my flesh
Cleanse my heart, heal my heart
Cleanse my mind, heal my mind
That I may be made whole.

When the Druid has bathed well in the waters, he sets them aside and takes up the prepared Blessing Fire. This should be a true open flame of some sort, such as camphor or small bits of firestarter, and small amounts of the three herbs should be to hand. Using vision and breath she accumulates the Heavens Power in herself and in the unlit

Blessing Fire. The focuses the light strongly into her hand and transfers into the Fire as she kindles it from the sacred Fire, saying:

I kindle this fire, a fire of magic, a shining of strength.

I kindle this fire, a fire of beauty, a warming of love

I kindle this fire, a fire of comfort,

A blessing of wholeness

A blessing of rightness, a blessing of healing

That wounds of the flesh be healed

(give the plantain)

That wounds of the heart be healed

(give St John's wort)

That wounds of the spirit be healed

(Give the vervain)

I charge you, oh fire, by the Fire of May

By the Fire in the Inner Grove

By the Fire in the Center of the Worlds.

Heal with your light, shining bright

Heal with your heat, warm and sweet

Body and soul, well and whole

Fire of Healing, Shine in me!

The Druid repeats the four-line charm as he lifts the Fire before him and warms his body with it. He lifts it before forehead, heart and loins in turn, and envisions the Fire reflected in his own form. He allows the Heaven power to fill him, driving away ill, filling and brightening shadows, perfecting and restoring the order of his being. When he has finished with the fire, he should set it down in front on him, making sure it is burning or smoking, and place the Water to its left. The Druid brings the Two Powers into gentle and powerful balance in herself, letting her right and left hands touch or reflect the blessings, as she says.

Let bound be bound and wound be wound,

And thus it is done, and done, and well done,

By the power of the Powers, and by my magic

So be it!

7: Closing

As usual.

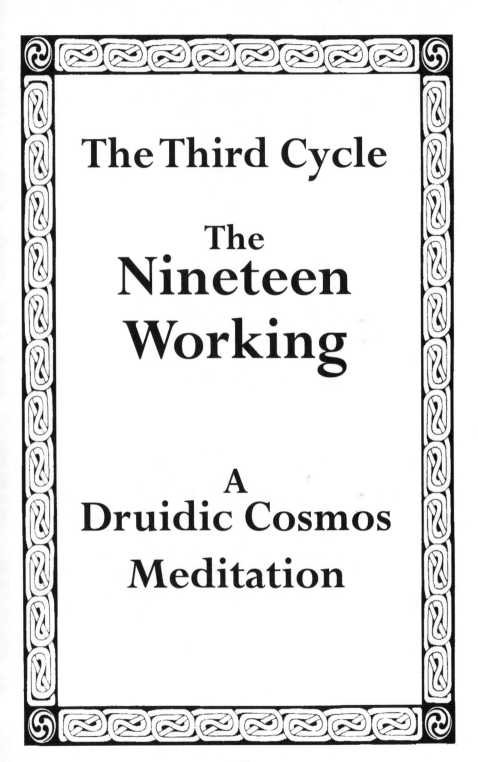

The Third Cycle

The
Nineteen Working

A
Druidic Cosmos
Meditation

The Third Cycle - Coming to the Center

The work of magic is the work of power. Power means many things. Power is ability - to have power is to be able. The magician's power comes first from ability, from strength and skill developed by practice. Complex visions such as the Nineteen Working exercise the mind and teach the student to remain calm and centered even in the face of cosmic vision.

In the Two Powers cycle the student begins reaching outside of himself for sources of greater power. In this cycle that outreach is continued, but also reversed. After opening the personal mind to contemplation of the greater cosmos, the two are then made one, the person made equal to the cosmos in vision. Thus, this technique both expands the mind into the greater reality, and brings the powers of that reality into the personal self.

This working is very useful as a stand-alone contemplation. Once the symbols are learned well it should be possible to complete the creation of the pattern, and then to abide within it in Open Meditation, allowing the cosmos to flow as the mind is still. However the Nineteen Working is also quite powerful both as a preliminary meditation before conjuring and as a place of power from which to greet the spirits. To be wrapped in the cosmic mandala before the spirits is to be visible as the God In You, vested with the authority proper to one who would be a player in the game of the spirit worlds.

The Nineteen Working is focused inside a Gaelic-based cosmology. To that base we add Indo-European patterns to fill out the picture and make a full cosmic diagram. As always, we do not have any traditional Gaelic Pagan cosmology handed down clearly from tradition. The pattern assembled here does bring together reliably Irish symbols, preserved in the poetic literature of the Middle Ages. The over-arching model of cosmos is drawn more broadly from cross-cultural mythic patterns.

This is probably the most ambitious work in this collection. Many people would be inclined to learn it by starting at the end and performing the whole sequence, repeating until you gain comprehension. However the chapter is arranged so that each section can be practiced in turn, one added to the next, until the pattern is complete. I strongly advise practicing each stage in turn. This will provide a much deeper experience than can be easily achieved by trying to grasp the whole working at once. The notes assume that one month is spent on each stage, but even working them over the course of a week, adding one stage each day, or in a once weekly practice would be of some benefit.

The Nineteen Working
A Druidic Work of Mystical Meditation

This working is intended to be done entirely in meditative posture, seated in whatever seat the Druid most commonly uses for trance and meditation. It is written to be done before the shrine or Hallows, or at least with real fire or incense and water, but once mastered can also be performed internally almost anywhere.

In terms of categories in world mysticism, this is a form of the Beatific Vision. It begins in the simple quiet of the personal mind. It progressively adds symbolism from the Celtic sacred cosmos, identifying the personal spirit with the spiritual reality of the worlds. Finally it offers a detailed presence of sacred reality within context of a mental discipline that seeks the truth of both the self and the world.

The work has five phases of mental focus, each with a specific psycho-spiritual intention. The first phase is so-called 'Open' Meditation, by which I mean the deliberate relaxation of attention away from the flow of normal thought. Open Meditation is suggested as the daily practice of the student in this work. The Druid learns that the point of attention... the inward I... is not based upon or dependent on the common flow of thoughts and feelings that usually drives our 'choices'. Rather there is a faculty of observation, an ability to observe ourselves 'from above' that transcends our common thoughts, emotions and preferences. When we have that state at our command we can always step aside from the rush of our reactions, to look upon evens, people and ourselves more dispassionately. In this, our basic practice serves the Druidic search for Truth. From that position of balance and calm we can face even the greatest Gods or demons.

The second phase of this work is the awareness of the core powers and structures of the cosmos. The Two Powers are a basic principle of our practical spiritual work. In this work we learn to use them swiftly and easily, though this mystical exercise doesn't deal with practical magical aspects. We balance the Two within the horizontal-axis knotwork of the Three Realms and Four Airts. Using these powerful symbols brings a balance and order to our internal world, just as ritual does to the external world. The web of influences of the Three and the Four keep the Two flowing into form, maintaining the cycle of growth, death and rebirth. Building this pattern in ourselves brings all these powers into the personal spirit.

The third phase of the work is self-awareness, and the understanding of our place and work in the world. The Three Cauldrons are each an expression of how the divine is expressed in each of us. Each of us has a unique web of connections and experiences, which go to feed the Cauldrons of each individual. The Cauldron meditations are a chance to look fearlessly at our own lives, to be open to the obvious and to the subtle, and to the highest as well as the lowest portions of our nature. The Druid should try to keep her attention balanced between the Three, even though inclination will tend to pull toward one trait, or away from another. The lore of the Irish Poets says that it is often the sudden great flood of emotion that brings a flow of insight or intuition that 'turns' a Cauldron to admit the flow of power. We hope to accomplish the same through the steady application of wisdom and effort.

The fourth phase is the work of opening the personal spirit to its identity with the cosmos, and with the land. The work of the Duile (Elements) is to affirm that the stuff of our existence is the stuff of all existence. We are not separate from stars and stones, even as we stand as distinct entities. In fact, when we relax our decision to be separate, we can find ourselves becoming one being, one spirit, with the cosmos itself. In this place we may find we have access to resources and experiences far beyond those of our personal spirit. Some say that the moment when the personal self becomes dissolved in the All That Is could be called 'enlightenment'.

The fifth phase brings us to the most speculative moment in this series of exercises. In this phase we return to the personal as we open to the Divine In Me. This Inner or Personal Divine Presence might be conceived of as a sort of Holy Guardian Angel, or as the AgathoDaimon, as the Fylgja or Hamingja, or as the Imbas or Awen. It is That In Us that will someday have the potential to receive worship and give blessing as an Ancestor. If that worship is to be our fate after death, how much better is it to seek that Power in our lives while we live?

The working will be presented in gradual stages. The student will be best served by taking each stage in turn, practicing it until fluent and then moving on to the next stage. The stages are meant to be cumulative, each building on the one before, but students may find one or another section useful as separate exercises, or may find they wish to change the order of the work. In this I would only suggest that the opening small rite and accompanying open meditation not be skipped, and be used as the foundation for any variation in the practices. Please understand that while I present my own words as bits of proper poetry for the intentions of the work, they are not, themselves, 'magic words' that will bring about the effects we seek. This is a work of mental focus and discipline. It requires repetition and intention from the outset. In every case the intention is to expand the awareness of the Druid, to deepen personal understanding, clarify the mind and build mental skills for further work.

Finally, for those who have the skill and discipline to succeed in working all five phases together into one great pattern, there is a great goal. This working intends to expand awareness – to carry the field of attention of the individual mind far beyond normal daily concerns and focuses. It intends to grant a Druidic version of the Beatific Vision – the perfect, holy cosmos - all arrayed around, beyond and within the soul of the Druid. In the secret center of that great pattern may be found an access to the Da Fein – to the Divine In Me – the oracle of the divine within the whirling pattern of the Dance of All Things. When the Druid becomes aware of her own Da Fein, and becomes aware of the unity of her Inner Vision with the Cosmos itself, then her Inner Divinity becomes one with the minds and power of the Gods Themselves, and with their awareness, across time and event. This awareness we might call a form of Druidic Illumination, perhaps even enlightenment. As always in these matters, from that point it becomes a matter of what wisdom the Druid may have, to live with the knowledge he might gain.

A Program for Working the Pattern

Weeks 1&2: Practice of Basic Shrine and Open meditation only. Daily practice is recommended, but at least three or four days per week can be sufficient.

Weeks 3&4: Maintain Basic work, add work with the Two Powers at least weekly, preferably more, until able to grasp them quickly and surely. Work the Four Airts attunement for experience.

Weeks 4 – 8: Basic work, with the Two Powers and the Worlds done with the Kindling Charm. During this time work with the Three Cauldrons as an exercise separate from the daily work.

Weeks 8 – 12: The Three Cauldrons exercise is added to the work.

As the exercise grows more complex you may choose to limit the full Pattern to Retreat days, while maintaining the Basic and Kindling Charm for daily work. During this month you may wish to work the Elements Charm as a separate exercise in preparation for the next phase.

Months 4 - 5: The Duile work added to the full pattern. Again this full work might be limited to Retreat days, but more frequent practice is recommended. During this time experimentation with the Da Fein.

Months 6 – 9: The Da Fein work is added to the full pattern, worked at least on the quarters. Daily work should come to include as much of the full Pattern as can be done skillfully and swiftly. Full skill is to be able to call the full pattern of awareness of All the Worlds about yourself in a sweep of vision, and place the Secret God shining in the center.

The Work Presented In Stages.
1: Simple Blessing & Open Meditation

In the course of working with students I find a continuing resistance to the systematic practice of basic Open Meditation. By this term I mean the practice of sitting motionless, concentrating attention on a single object, such as the breath, while allowing other thought and sensation to flow by the attention without attachment. This technique is basic to further trance and even to ritual work and should be a common part of any program of mental practice for magic. Beginning students, however, do find reasons to balk.

Some seem to find the business of sitting motionless, pursuing nothing except mental action to be tedious and challenging. Often students approach meditation as if the intention were to 'stop thinking'. In some systems, indeed, this does seem to be a goal, with great value placed on finding and enhancing the silence between thoughts. Druidic lore doesn't suggest that as, in itself, a core goal. It seems to occur spontaneously in some students, but it isn't central to the work.

Rather the point of this method for the system we're building is the development of a detached observer in the self – a point of observation for all that passes, within or without. The student learns to maintain her equanimity – engage her passions at need and to step away when she must. The work of Pagan spiritual practice can arouse the passions, can stir up ones mental contents. The ability to stand in a place of neutrality and peace offers a special strength in the work of magic, whether it's dealing with one's emotions, or facing the Gods.

It is common to confuse basic trance with the work of Open Meditation. They are, in fact, closely related, but there is an important distinction. Basic trance is the primary mental preparation, induced by relaxing the body, focusing the attention and suspending critical observation (or 'attachment' as some say). We have taught this state through the Fire and Water induction, and the Bone, Breath and Blood exercise. Either of those exercises, among many other similar forms, produces the focused poise that leads to other trance states.

Open Meditation can be understood as an extension of that poise into a longer experience sustained by will. By directing the concentration upon a single focus – watching the breath being our most usual method – we locate the still point around which our ongoing thoughts can flow. As our thoughts and impressions flow around us, we keep returning our awareness to the focus as we sit in stillness. By sustaining the relaxation, concentration and detachment of basic trance we allow the mind and emotions to relax in turn, releasing the 'knots and kinks' of daily life.

Open meditation is an excellent accompaniment to the regular work of ritual purification. The Water and Fire clear away the spiritual cobwebs and parasites of daily spiritual life in the world. Open meditation deprives your personal inner imps and larvae of their food and weakens their grip.

So we begin the formal work of mental training by learning to abide calmly among our own thoughts and feelings. If no other good were gained from the work of Druidry, the ability to stand at peace amid the swirl of life's impulses would pay for all. In order to work the system I'm presenting here the student will have to simply choose to set to it, and develop the basic skills that support all further work. We will refer often to the 'Druid's Peace" in this work – by this we mean that steady and unmoved center. In addition to this Peace, we will learn a set of active meditations, but the Peace is the basis of them all, because the Peace grants access to the management of the mind by will.

Open meditation is as basic to mental training as aerobic exercise is to training the body. Some students will take to it readily, others may find it more difficult. Its value and results speak for themselves and to neglect it in early training is to deprive yourself of future resources.

Working Open Meditation

1: Find your seat, in a position that can be comfortably maintained with your spine straight. Begin patterned breathing. Work the Blood, Breath and Bone induction. If you wish to work a simple shrine opening, do so now. Practice maintaining basic trance as you speak and do the ritual gestures. Return to motionless basic trance following the work.

2: Choose a point of focus for your concentration. Initially you should continue to use the breath.

• With your attention focused simply sit and maintain that focus. You choose not to give attention to any specific thought that arises, whether about the object of concentration or any other thing. Each time that you notice a thought or specific impression holding your attention, return your attention to the focus. That is the entire basic technique. Like raising an arm or taking a step it is the act of will that brings the attention back to the focus.

• As you practice you will begin to notice more quickly when you have drifted, and be able to hold your concentration on the focus for longer without breaks. This is the first level of success in this practice.

3: Always end the session of meditation formally, with the recitation of a closing charm and/or other formal gesture.

Stage 1 Practice:
Simple Shrine Blessing and Open Meditation.

This first section can always serve as a fall-back, or minimum practice. It can be done daily, even as you add additional work during retreats or more focused workings.

The Druid seats himself in her seat, facing east if possible. If there can be hallowed Fire and Water, so much the better. The body should be kept balanced and alert, while relaxed.

Begin your breathing pattern. Find your peace, perhaps using the Bone, Breath and Blood method.

Bless the Water and Fire, as you say:

The Fire, the Well, the Sacred Tree
Flow and Flame and Grow in me
In Land, Sea and Sky, Below and on High,
Let the Water be blessed and the Fire be hallowed.

When you are ready, dip your hand in the Water and sprinkle or lave yourself, then pass your hands through the incense or Fire and bring it onto yourself, as you say:

By the Might of the Waters and the Light of the Fire
Cleansed of ill and bane am I
By the Might of the Waters and the Light of the Fire
Blessed in Land and Sea and Sky

As you cleanse and bless yourself, feel the Water and Fire washing and searing away all that's not in your true pattern of being.

Light an additional offering of incense, and open your heart in welcome to all the Holy Beings. Say:

Gods and Dead and Mighty Sidhe
Powers of Earth and Sky and Sea
By Fire and Well, by Sacred Tree
Welcome I do give to ye.

At this time you may wish to pause in open meditation for as long as you wish. In daily practice it can be enough to do the simple cleansing, followed by open meditation.

When your meditative practice is complete, take time to return your awareness fully and completely to your body and material senses. Even as you remember what you may have gained or learned in a working, allow your awareness to return to common life and breath. Before you rise from your seat pause for a moment and return to your center in peace. Cross your hands on your chest and say:

The blessings of the Holy Ones be on me and mine
My blessings on all beings, with peace on thee and thine
The Fire, the Well, the Sacred Tree
Flow and Flame and Grow in me
Thus do I remember the work of the Wise.

2: Energy Work The Vertical Axis

The second stage of our pattern begins with the work called 'grounding and centering". In that technique we make ourselves aware of a flow of "spiritual energies" in the cosmos, and balance those energies in our own bodies and spirits. We 'ground' ourselves by connecting personal reality with a much larger system that can both empower and backup our own work and we 'center' ourselves by organizing the flow of energies in ourselves in a symmetrical and balanced way.

There is a serious discussion to be had about how the ancients might have viewed this concept of 'spiritual energy', and whether it occurred at all among the Celts. We see a clear model of it in yogic systems from India, and techniques from that cultural range had a wide distribution among the Wise. There are traces in Irish vocabulary that are suggestive, but we must plainly say that we are adapting a modern magical technique to our Druidic cosmology when we use the Two Powers as 'energies in the body'.

In the work of Our Druidry we address these energies as the Light of the Heavens and the Waters of the Underworld. The Underworld Power is envisioned as the Waters Under the Earth, in which all the wisdom of the past is dissolved. The Power of the heavens is seen as the Light of the Turning Sky, which brings order, pattern and growth. This duality corresponds to cosmic principles, poles of cosmic structure between which the manifest world appears. They reflect a core Celtic cosmological division of the cosmos into two – Fire and Water, Summer and Winter, Day and Night. Of course such a duality is not a moral opposition – summer and winter are lovers as well as warring knights. This work, like all of the work that follows, is in one way a contemplation of the powers and components of our cosmology. By making the macrocosm of the Sacred Cosmos real in our own spirits we hope to gain in personal understanding, and in the spiritual authority that allows us to interact with the Gods as beings of worth.

Working with the Fire and Water is a core technique of Druidic practical magic, but it also serves as a method of spiritual development.

Contemplation of the Two Powers begins the process of expanding the personal mind into transpersonal mythic spaces. The Fire and Water are the primal powers of creation. When we take conscious control of the Two Powers, through imagination and will, we are doing in the microcosm what the Gods and Spirits do in the greater cosmos.

The pattern of symbolic meditation based on the Two Powers begins the recapitulation of the mythic cosmos. In the work of Open Meditation we begin with the Unformed, the Chaos from which order arises. With the Two Powers energy-work we begin the process of manifestation, with the appearance of the core Indo-European duality of Fire and Water.

The practical goal of this stage of energy-work (which was begun, we hope, in the Dedicant's work) is to learn to bring (awareness of) the Two Powers into the self quickly and surely. In our Dedicant training we provided a detailed text induction. In this phase we learn to establish the flow of the Powers with a will and a few breaths. The goal is to create a state in which the Light and the Shadow are flowing and shining in and through the body in a balanced but free-flowing way. From that base any number of specialized forms and applications of the energies can be devised.

In order to be able to spend working time on actual goals, rather than on inductions, the student must learn to find the balanced poise of the Two Powers in a swift and easy way. If you have worked with the Nine Breaths technique, you will be prepared to move to the Three Breaths method. The Kindling Charm is meant to train the body/mind to bring the Powers into balance with the simple recitation of a charm, accompanied by gesture. As you learn the method you may choose to speak the charm slowly, to the rhythm of three breaths. As you gain experience you will be able to bring the desired balanced energy-state with even a quick recitation of the charm, or with an act of will alone.

It's simple to describe the basic practice:

1: Induce basic trance

2: Conceive yourself seated or standing between the Deep Waters and the Wheel of Stars.

3: Realize your connection with the Waters Beneath. With a single long, complete breath bring the Deep Power into your whole body.

4: Realize your connection with the Fire Above. With a single long, complete breath bring the Sky Power into your whole body.

5: Circulate the Two with a third deep breath.

At this level we expect students to be able to lead themselves in the work, remembering and applying each stage as directed. Thus we haven't provided formal 'scripting' for the use of the Two Powers with the Kindling Charm, though there are a couple of audio files of guided meditation-style inductions available on the disk that acoompanies this text.

Three Worlds and Four Quarters

The next phase of the exercise – expressed very simply in a short charm – is the establishment in the mind of the pattern of the manifest world – the Three Worlds and Four Directions. The Two Powers are the 'vertical axis' – rooted deep and crowned high. Around this spindle of light and shadow the Wheel of the World turns.

In our Celtic system we see the 'horizontal axis' – the plane of the Middle World – as divided both three-fold and four-fold. First we see the manifest world divided into Land, Sea and Sky. These are the primal Celtic (and IndoEuropean) division of the manifest world. In this pattern the land is the world-island on which our lives are grounded. Surrounding the Land is the Ocean-Sea, the all-encompassing salt waters, and over all the dome of the Sky holds the turning lights.

In this vision you stand in the center of this mythic triad, in the center of the Land in the Center of the Worlds, as it were. The Land itself is further divided with the cross of the Four Directions. While many systems use a quartered circle, ours does not employ the hermetic 'elements' of fire, water, air and earth. In this work we use the symbolism of the four Irish provinces, the various paths and stations of human life, distilled into simple terms in the charm.

The ritual text presented below conjures the vision of the vertical axis in just a few words. We also provide some more detailed exercises . If possible it is best to get out under the sky, to stand or sit perhaps upon a hilltop or a rise and work the exercises in a place where the real horizon and forms of the Land can be seen. The impressions and memories from those exercises will bring depth when you work the quick version of the charm.

The Four Airts Attunement

This exercise can be worked separately as an attunement to the Quarters, or it can be added to the full script, replacing the simple charm of the four directions.

• Taking up the Slat if you wish, or using a pointing hand, turn to the East. Make an invoking spiral, spiraling out deisil from the center to the edge of the spiral. Say:

East wind blow Bounty

• Envision a red wind blowing from the east into your spirit, bringing with it awareness of the power of growth and wealth in your life. Feel that wind filling places in your life that might be 'empty' of the power of prosperity.

• Turn to the South and make the invoking spiral, saying:

South wind blow Song

• Envision a white wind blowing from the south, bringing awareness of wildness and the outsiders into your spirit. Feel that outsider wind stir and shake the order of your existence, bringing new impulse and energy.

• Turn to the West and make the invoking spiral, saying:

West wind blow Wisdom

• Envision a twilight-gray wind blowing into your spirit from the west, bringing with it knowledge and inspiration. Feel that wind blow into empty places in your mind, bringing cleverness and understanding.

• Turn to the North and make the invoking spiral, saying:

North wind blow Strong

• Envision a black wind blowing into your spirit from the north, bringing with it strength and. Feel the wind filling the places in your heart that need it, bringing vigor and honor.

• Return to your Peace, and allow the vision to fade, or continue with the conclusion of any greater exercise.

Stage 2 Practice: Shrine and Meditation, With the Two, the Three and the Four

Begin your breathing pattern. Find your peace, perhaps using the Bone, Breath and Blood method.

Bless the Water and Fire, as you say:

The Fire, the Well, the Sacred Tree
Flow and Flame and Grow in me
In Land, Sea and Sky, Below and on High,
Let the Water be blessed and the Fire be hallowed.

When you are ready, dip your hand in the Water and sprinkle or lave yourself, then pass your hands through the incense or Fire and bring it onto yourself, as you say:

By the Might of the Waters and the Light of the Fire
Cleansed of ill and bane am I
By the Might of the Waters and the Light of the Fire
Blessed in Land and Sea and Sky

At this time you may wish to pause in open meditation for as long as you wish. After you have found your Peace, resume your center and bring the Two Powers into yourself, swiftly allowing the Waters to rise, followed by the descent of the Light, as you do the Kindling Charm:

Cross your hands on your chest and say:

Powers of the Earth and Sky
Rooted deep and crowned high

Place fingers on forehead, chest and loins in turn, bringing the Two Powers smoothly into each, saying

Flow and kindle in my head
Flow and kindle in my heart
Flow and kindle in my loins

Cross your hands on your chest, feeling the balanced flow of the Two, and say:

Flow and shine in every part.

Remain with hands crossed on the chest or, if you prefer, extend your arms straight from your shoulders, as you say:

The Land upholds me, the Sea surrounds me,
the Sky above me.
Before me bounty, behind me wisdom
On my right hand magic, on my left hand strength

Cross hands again on the chest

For the Cauldron is in me.

And I am seated in the Center of Worlds.

At this time you may wish to pause in a Contemplation Meditation in which you compose yourself seating in the center of the Worlds and Realms, with all the Powers at your hand. This meditation can be maintained as long as you wish, simply experiencing the feel of the Pattern of the Worlds around you, with the Fire and Water in you. When you have finished your meditation practice you should make a simple offering to the Spirits. Light an additional offering of incense, and open your heart in welcome to all the Holy Beings. Say:

Gods and Dead and Mighty Sidhe

Powers of Earth and Sky and Sea

By Fire and Well, by Sacred Tree

Offering I give to ye.

Take time to return your awareness fully and completely to your body and material senses. Even as you remember what you may have gained or learned, allow your awareness to return to common life and breath. Before you rise from your seat, pause for a moment and return to your center in peace. Cross your hands on your chest and say:

The blessings of the Holy Ones be on me and mine

My blessings on all beings,

with peace on thee and thine

The Fire, the Well, the Sacred Tree

Flow and Flame and Grow in me

Thus do I remember the work of the Wise.

3: Using the Three Cauldrons

In the very small list of remnants of Celtic culture that suggest actual Pagan mysticism or spiritual symbolism the complex of the Three Cauldrons stands out plainly. Based on the medieval Irish poem the Cauldron of Poesy, we describe three Cauldrons or "boiling places" in the human system, into which the Power of Inspiration can flow and be held. The Cauldrons in each individual may be either empty, half-full or full, and by this is determined how much poetic or spiritual power the individual possesses.

The Three Cauldrons are described as:

1: The Cauldron of Warming, conceived of as located in the belly, is the source of physical and constitutional health and strength. It is born upright in all people, with the potential to be fully filled.

2: The Cauldron of Motion or 'Vocation', is conceived of as in the heart. It is the core of the poet's vision and work, the place where he receives his actual skill and inspiration. It is born in most tipped on its side, able to hold only a portion of the flow.

"The cauldron of motion then, in all artless people is on its lips. It is side-slanting in people of bardcraft and small poetic talent. It is upright in the greatest of poets, who are great streams of wisdom. Not every poet has it on its back, for the cauldron of motion must be turned by sorrow or joy."

3: The Cauldron of Wisdom is conceived of as in the head. It is the container of the highest spiritual and artistic inspirations. It grants not just poetry but 'every art'.

The central metaphor for spiritual power or wisdom in the Cauldron of Poesy is Poetic Inspiration. The poet's ability to produce inspired verse is also his ability to make magic. Throughout this work we will use the metaphor of poetic skill and inspiration as the equivalent of spiritual and magical power, and we will work toward the use of poetry as a core element of ritual and spellbinding.

The majority of the text of the Cauldron of Poesy focuses on the Cauldron of Motion as the vessel that truly holds the poets power. It is born half-tipped, and it is by the deeds and events of human life that it becomes fully upright, able to obtain a full measure of the Mead of Wisdom. In the same way the Cauldron of Wisdom is born tipped on its lip, empty of power, and must be turned. This is described as happening due to powerful emotional events - sorrows and joys - during the course of life.

The Four Sorrows: longing, grief, jealousy and hard travel.

The Joys are said to be twofold: divine joy and human joy. Human joy is

64

fourfold: Sexual delight, physical health, the joy of prosperity from one's vocation, the joy of success in one's efforts. Divine joys are the delight of the Blessings of the Gods, and the joy of eating of the Hazels of the Well of Wisdom, as it is said.

These joys and sorrows come from the events of our lives – they are not just from within, but rather they must grow from real experience and relationship with the other. In a modern life, if we have any adventure in us at all, any of that which might make a poet or magician, we will have many of the joys and sorrows described. If we can take them in, process them, boil them up, they become the raw material for our understanding and wisdom.

So in this exercise we use the Cauldrons as anchoring symbols for a wide range of contemplations, focused on our own bodies, lives and spiritual growth. In order to comprehend and digest the joys and sorrows of our lives we contemplate them in formal meditation. By bringing the memory of the events before the mind's vision, while maintaining the detached perspective of Open Meditation we can process them effectively. So we contemplate in turn the body, the network of our 'professional' life, and our spiritual condition.

There's a word to be said about the presentation of the Cauldron of Motion. In the original poem the heart cauldron is plainly related to the poets life and livelihood, on the deeds that bring inspiration and the rewards of poetic success. For those of us who approach the work intending to be a poet-seer in the old ways, we can simply proceed. For those of us who may have different path in life, whether the warrior or the merchant or another profession, there's no reason why wisdom and inspiration won't serve equally well. So we have tweaked the work of the Cauldron of Motion to be more broadly applicable to the 'vocation' of whoever might undertake the work.

Fó topar tomseo,
fó atrab n-insce,
fó comair coimseo
con-utaing firse.
Good is the well of poetry,
good is the dwelling of speech,
good is the union of power and mastery
which establishes strength.

Stage Three Practice: Adding the Cauldrons
1: Simple Shrine Blessing.

Bless the Water and Fire, as you say:

The Fire, the Well, the Sacred Tree

Flow and Flame and Grow in me

In Land, Sea and Sky, Below and on High,

Let the Water be blessed and the Fire be hallowed.

Sprinkle or lave yourself, then pass your hands through the incense or Fire as you say:

By the Might of the Waters and the Light of the Fire

Cleansed of ill and bane am I

By the Might of the Waters and the Light of the Fire

Blessed in Land and Sea and Sky

Light an additional offering of incense, and open your heart in welcome to all the Holy Beings. Say:

Gods and Dead and Mighty Sidhe

Powers of Earth and Sky and Sea

By Fire and Well, by Sacred Tree

Welcome I do give to ye.

At this time you may wish to pause in open meditation for a short while,

2: Two Powers, Three Realms, Four Airts
Cross your hands on your chest and say:

Powers of the Earth and Sky

Rooted deep and crowned high

Place fingers on forehead, chest and loins in turn, bringing the Two Powers smoothly into each, saying

Flow and kindle in my head

Flow and kindle in my heart

Flow and kindle in my loins

Cross your hands on your chest, feeling the balanced flow of the Two, and say:

Flow and shine in every part.

Remain with hands crossed on the chest or, if you prefer, extend your arms straight from your shoulders.

The Land upholds me, the Sea surrounds me, the Sky above me.

Before me bounty, behind me wisdom
On my right hand magic, on my left hand strength
Cross hands again on the chest
For the Cauldron is in me.
And I am seated in the Center of Worlds.
At this time you establish a contemplation in which you are seated in the center of the Worlds and Realms, with all the Powers at your hand.

3: The Three Cauldrons
The Two Powers are settled into a clear flow in the self, and the Druid begins to focus them into the Three Cauldrons Attunement:
With the Two Powers established in your body, establish the Three Cauldrons, beginning with your loins.
Envision the Cauldron of Warming low in your belly, see it made of iron, or stone heated by the fire below. Intone the name:

Goriath (goh ree ah)
Envision the combined Light and Shadow flowing into your Cauldron of Warming. As it does, open your awareness to your body. Become aware of your flesh and bone, blood and belly and brain, seeking an awareness of your health and wholeness, and, by will, seeing yourself as hale and well in every part.

Envision the Cauldron of Vocation in the heart. See it made of silver and gold, heated be the fire in your heart. Intone the name:

Ernmas (air'n mahs)
Let the Powers flow into the Cauldron of Movement, and feel your awareness open to your daily life and work, to the deeds and events of your life. Become aware of your place in the world, among kin and folk and the wide world. From the center that is the Cauldron see the webs of relationship and mutuality that hold your life together. See them made strong, whole and helpful.

Envision the Cauldron of Wisdom in your head. See it made of crystal and amber, lit and warmed by the fire above. Intone the name:

Sofhis (so wish)
Let the Two Powers flow into the Cauldron of Wisdom, and open your spirit to your spiritual way and work. As the Fire and Water fill the Cauldron open your mind to the sources of divine awareness in your life. Feel your Allies draw close, and the Divine In You shine and flow, filling you with the Mead of Inspiration.

As you wish, and as you are able, let your mind rest in balance between these three Cauldrons. Broaden your attention to allow the three sets of images to flow and intertwine. In this weaving there may be things to be learned. Understand that these Cauldrons are always in you, always turned or turning, just as the Two Powers always flow in you. Rest and work in this state as long as you like.

4: Closing

Take time to return your awareness fully and completely to your body and material senses. Even as you remember what you may have gained or learned, allow your awareness to return to common life and breath. Before you rise from your seat, pause for a moment and return to your center in peace. Cross your hands on your chest and say:

The blessings of the Holy Ones be on me and mine
My blessings on all beings,
with peace on thee and thine
The Fire, the Well, the Sacred Tree
Flow and Flame and Grow in me
Thus do I remember the work of the Wise.

4: The Duile – Microcosm and Macrocosm

The principle that the greater world (in Irish, bith - 'what is') - both material and spiritual - is reflected in the personal body and spirit of the individual is an Indo-European universal. "As above, so below; and as below, so above" the old aphorism says, and we can find plenty of evidence for the principle in Irish lore. The Irish poems describe a correspondence between the parts of the natural world and the parts of the human body and mind. These parts are called the duile, which means 'elements' or 'components'. There are several traditional lists of these symbols. We will adopt a ninefold model similar to those current in Neopagan Celtic circles.

- **Crown of the Head - Starry Heavens**
- **Brains - Clouds**
- **Face - Sun**
- **Mind - Moon**
- **Breath - Wind**
- **Blood - Sea**
- **Hair - Plants**
- **Flesh - Soil**
- **Bone – Stone**

We can, with a little flexibility, divide these into the Three Worlds so that:
Land: Plants, Soil and Stone
Sea: Clouds, Wind and Sea
Sky: Heavens, Moon, and Sun.

The source of these correspondences, in the misty past of Indo-European origins, is said to be the myth of the First Sacrifice, in which the First Cosmic Being is offered, or offers itself, on the altar. From the death of that First Being, and from its body and spirit, the cosmos itself is created. In some versions of the tale this is also the beginning of the work of sacrifice itself, in other versions the Killing is more like war or murder, but in every case the world is then made from the bones, blood, breath and mind.

This being the case it is true to say that, regardless of our form, we are all made of one substance. From Gods to gardens, from ourselves to the stars and stones, we are all made of the Holy Flesh of the First Sacrifice. This is the archaic root of the later metaphysical doctrines of the Hermeticists, and the macrocosm/microcosm complex seems as Gaelic as it is renaissance Italian.

In the previous stages of this work we have created a Sacred Pattern of the cosmos - the Two, the Three and the Four, and focused and channeled the world's flow into our own bodies and lives with the Cauldrons. In this stage we seek to realize the unity of our personal existence with the greater existence of the worlds. Our flesh is the flesh of the world, our spirits are the spirit of the world – and so is everything else.

Most importantly, from a mystical perspective, our personal spiritual nature is, at the deepest point, still one with the spiritual nature that infuses the whole of existence. The First Person became Impersonal Mind, by dying, and by living, we participate in that Mind. By entering deep into our own awareness, by moving past layers of common thought and focusing on patterns of holy symbol, we hope to have the experience of the all-mind, to expand awareness beyond our self and name, beyond our apparent flesh into the mind and flesh of the Divine World.

As in the previous stage, in this exercise you will build the pattern of vision, and then spend time in contemplation of the pattern. This stage becomes rather different – it is relaxing, opening and dissolving to the constructed self, where before the work had been about consciously constructing and using the pattern of self. You may find your complex of Fire and Water, Worlds and Quarters dissolving into the pattern of the world, or you may simply leave it behind for a time as your awareness expands past its limits. In any case upon finishing the meditation on the whole pattern, and opening up to the oneness with the Elements, you will return to your pattern of Two, Three and Four, with the Cauldrons, before closing the work.

Stage 4 Practice: The Elements of the Worlds
1: Simple Shrine Blessing.

Bless the Water and Fire, as you say:

The Fire, the Well, the Sacred Tree
Flow and Flame and Grow in me
In Land, Sea and Sky, Below and on High,
Let the Water be blessed and the Fire be hallowed.

Sprinkle or lave yourself, then pass your hands through the incense or Fire and bring it onto yourself, say:

By the Might of the Waters and the Light of the Fire
Cleansed of ill and bane am I
By the Might of the Waters and the Light of the Fire
Blessed in Land and Sea and Sky

Cleanse and bless yourself, feel the Water and Fire washing and searing away all that's not in your true pattern of being. Light an additional offering of incense, and open your heart in welcome to all the Holy Beings. Say:

Gods and Dead and Mighty Sidhe
Powers of Earth and Sky and Sea
By Fire and Well, by Sacred Tree
Welcome I do give to ye.

At this time you may wish to pause in open meditation.

2: Two Powers, Three Realms, Four Airts

The Kindling Charm:

Cross your hands on your chest and say:

Powers of the Earth and Sky
Rooted deep and crowned high

Place fingers on forehead, chest and loins in turn, saying

Flow and kindle in my head
Flow and kindle in my heart
Flow and kindle in my loins

Cross your hands on your chest, and say:

Flow and shine in every part.

Remain with hands crossed on the chest or, if you prefer, extend your arms straight from your shoulders, say:

The Land upholds me, the Sea surrounds me,
the Sky above me.
Before me bounty, behind me wisdom
On my right hand magic, on my left hand strength
Cross hands again on the chest
For the Cauldron is in me.
And I am seated in the Center of Worlds.
Pause in a meditation

Stage 3: The Three Cauldrons

Envision the Cauldron of Warming low in your belly, intone the name:

Goriath (goh ree ah)

Envision the combined Light and Shadow flowing into your Cauldron of Warming. Envision the Cauldron of Vocation in the heart. Intone the name:

Ernmas (air'n mahs)

Envision the Light and Shadow flowing into your Cauldron of Motion. Envision the Cauldron of Wisdom in your head. Intone the name:

Sofhis (so wish)

Let the Two Powers flow into the Cauldron of Wisdom. Let your mind rest in balance between these three Cauldrons as long as you like.

4: The Elements

Bring the Powers into balance in yourself, remembering your detachment, gently and firmly bringing the Two Powers and the Three Cauldrons into a balanced flow. Remember the vision of the Worlds, and become aware of your flesh and spirit as you work the Duile Attunement. By this charm you will turn your attention to the elements of the Worlds, one element at a time. As you are learning the exercise feel free to take each section slowly, meditating on the union, the co-substance, of your individual existence with the much greater world of All That Is.

Today I open myself
To the Elements of the World.
The first triad concerns the Land. Feel your solid flesh sharing its substance with the stones and roots and growing things of the Land, letting it become you, and you, it.
Eternal stone my bones.
My flesh the warm soil,
My hair the green bounty,

72

The second triad concerns the Sea. Feel the processes of your material life as interchangeable with the great ebbs and flows of the endless deep, letting it become you, and you, it.

The sea my blood,
My breath the wind,
Cool moonlight my mind,

The third triad concerns the Sky. Feel your reason and emotion and spirit shining and turning among your thoughts, like the eternal heavens. Let it become you, and you, it.

The sun my face,
My thoughts the clouds,
The stars behind my eyes.

Feel yourself vanishing into the world, and the world vanishing into you, but all the while, your core of Fire and Water, your Three Cauldrons, remain balanced and firm, even as your awareness opens.

All the world is in me,
And I am in the world.

4: Closing

Take time to return your awareness fully and completely to your body and material senses, and say:

The blessings of the Holy Ones be on me and mine
My blessings on all beings,
with peace on thee and thine
The Fire, the Well, the Sacred Tree
Flow and Flame and Grow in me
Thus do I remember the work of the Wise.

5: The Hidden God – the Da Fein

In a polytheistic spiritual system, it is possible to be bewildered by the crowd of spirits, of divine beings. Systems that posit a single deity make it easy, at least, to determine where to focus one's worship. In system where the model of the divine more closely mirrors the patterns of nature, the forest of possibilities can seem daunting.

Practical Paganism addresses this problem by the creation by individuals of personal pantheons. Each land, each people, each village, each family hearth, even each individual has a constellation of Gods and Spirits that best suits the needs of life and circumstances. For an ancient Pagan this process would have been a natural product of their upbringing. As modern Pagans, we must work our way from our 20th century upbringings. This can make the process much more conscious and artificial and, perhaps, more difficult.

It is important to be aware, from the outset, of the danger of importing prejudices learned from the common culture, or from our upbringing in other systems. One such subtle leftover is the tendency to reserve 'divinity' for only the highest and deepest of spiritual things. Christianity has demanded that worship be reserved only for 'the divine', and has limited divinity to their single 'God'. From another perspective, Buddhism and some kinds of Hinduism tend to define all manifest or social reality as 'illusion' and advise students to focus on the goal of liberation from that illusion, rejecting worship of any manifest thing. However in much of Hinduism, and certainly in its Vedic predecessor, this sort of doctrine just does not apply. In those more traditional forms 'liberation' is a venerable goal, but worship of 'lesser' beings is integral to the system.

This reservation of worship only to the highest or truest is clearly not part of core IE Pagan tradition. For example in Hellenic Paganism the term 'theos', which we commonly translate 'god', was used for any being that inspired awe and reverence. The term was applied to the Olympian deities, to mighty spirits of the land, to the heroes, and was even occasionally applied to mortal kings. Pagan systems tend to view divinity as intimately present in the manifest world. Divinity can't be limited to the 'highest' or 'truest'. For us the divine is part of the fabric of all existence, present in stone and stream, herb and tree, bird and beast. Thus, it must also be present in humankind.

Pagans seek the divine in many places. We address the Gods and Spirits, we find the divine in a tree or a stone. However, modern Pagans may find it difficult to consider honoring the spirit of a living human as divine – including, of course, ourselves. Some religious and cultural traditions teach that humans are intrinsically unworthy, weak, even depraved or evil, requiring an external divine intervention. Even in secular discourse it seems common to devalue our human nature. Perhaps this is a reaction to the sort of recent western arrogance that considers humankind to be the 'highest' of all creatures. In any case, the concept of the divine present in our own human nature is not a common one in our culture.

It seems to me that traditional IE Paganism neither devalued nor overestimated humankind. When the divine can be immanently present in beasts and stones, we cannot think ourselves superior to our environment. Yet humans who do great deeds – or who simply win the love and reverence of their kin - can become objects of worship. Certainly this may happen after death, as ancestors, but it may happen even while alive. The Roman custom of deifying the 'genius' – the personal divine spirit – of their emperors after death has been frequently criticized by Christian historians, but it is only a state example of a custom that might extend into any village.

So, we may suggest that we are within tradition when we acknowledge – even worship – the divine power in ourselves, and in one another. This may seem a radical notion to modern students. We commonly ask the Kindreds to join us in worship of one another, on the principle that all that is divine worships itself through its many beings. If we were to formally worship the 'God of Myself', along with the many gods, we might find ourselves asking the Powers to join us in that worship. Is this plain hubris?

In order to avoid it, we must remember that in such a formula we offer worship to our own divine core or crown, not merely to the personality and flesh that we commonly identify as 'me'. Just as when we offer to a tree we are not worshipping its cellulose and water, so we are not asking any being to worship our meat and mannerisms.

Once again, in a Pagan theology divinity does not mean 'omnipotent, omniscient owner-operator-of-the-cosmos'. It is only monotheism that attempts to restrict the divine to one being. For us, every existing thing partakes to some degree in the divine. That must, surely, include us.

As modern Pagans we can choose to make the crossing from viewing ourselves as mere flesh machines to viewing ourselves as multidimensional beings with the Divine Fire and water in us. It will be to our great advantage to recognize that in each of us there is a true Flame, a true Well of power and wisdom and love. Each of us contains, by right of birth, the divine.

So then, what is this divine portion of the human being? It is called by many names in many systems. In some Hindu thought it is called the atman.

Hindus greet one another with the traditional 'namaste' which means 'the divine in me greets the divine in you'. The Greeks spoke of the Agathodaimon – a spiritual voice in the self that gave access to wisdom. The Romans spoke of the 'genius', which has the connotation of 'family spirit' – the divine force in the self that allows us to become honored ancestors when our time comes. Some systems view this power as rather impersonal; others see it as an 'angel' or 'familiar spirit' that attends the mortal. Medieval ceremonialists and their modern inheritors have called it the 'Holy Guardian Angel', making that unnecessary distinction between the angelic and the divine.

We have no direct reference to such a principle in Celtic lore. We do have Celtic poetry that celebrates the eternal, ever-changing spirit of the human poets that made it. The most renowned of these, the Song of Amairgin, describes the Druid's self-perception as one with all of nature. It includes the famous line: "I am a God that fashions fire for a head". This image of 'fire in the head' has become a metaphor for poetic inspiration, which is, itself, the presence of the divine power in Celtic lore. The Celtic lore concerning the Cauldron of Wonder, remembered in later tales as the Holy Grail, also points at an impersonal divine power that is discovered by self-mastery and the solving of the riddles of personal will and fate.

If we have such a divine spirit in ourselves then making ourselves aware of that spirit and its capacities, and working with it consciously, seems a fine goal for those inclined to spiritual work. Socrates spoke of his daimon – the spirit that advised him in his deeds. Later theurges from Hellenic nations, and various yogis and rishis of the Indic peoples developed detailed methods of approaching one's internal divine power. We have no specific record of such things among the Pagan Celts – such practice would have reeked of sorcery or heresy to the monkish chroniclers. It does not seem unreasonable to suppose that Druids (who inherit the same traditions that produced the mysticism of other cultures) in the course of their searching into the world, would have sought contact with their own Divine nature.

As Pagans it is proper for us to honor the divine in every place that we find it. Thus it is reasonable for us to begin to learn how to worship out own divine nature, and those of the mortals around us. I cannot say, in this short musing, how such a doctrine may find expression in Our Paganism, but I have included a short poetic charm and exercise which could be added to personal devotions or ceremonies. I expect that the inspiration and genius of our folk will lead us to powerful expressions of this core Pagan idea.

May we come to know the spark and flow of the divine power in us all!

Stage 5 Practice: An Da Fein

If you are able to master your mind again, you may be able to bring all this to a balanced and ordered pattern in yourself. Use your detachment to prevent the awe of the work from overwhelming your will, and find, once again, your center. It is from this Center of All That Is that you can seek the Da Fein — the God of You. The Da Fein is a subtle concept, with many layers of symbolism. You can begin, in this simple exercise, with the symbols of the Light Above and the Light Below, or the falling of the Gold and Silver Drops of the Cauldron of Inspiration. In this symbol we seek the Druids' Treasure, the Celtic version of the Holy Grail, or the Philosopher's Stone, that perfects and empowers and illuminates. So choose a symbol to work with, perhaps varying them as you practice.

So, seated in balance in the Center of the Worlds, turn your attention to the point just above your nose, a point in a triangle with your two eyes. Turn your awareness into that point, as if it were a doorway, in toward the Center of the Center. Recite the charm as you contemplate the symbols it offers:

I am a kinsman of the Fire

I am a child of the Waters

My flesh is holy, born of the holy union

My Spirit is a drop of the Cauldron of Wonder,

A spark of the Divine Fire.

(Place a hand on the forehead)

The Divine Presence is in my head *(Place hand on heart)*

The Divine Presence is in my heart *(Place hand on the loins)*

The Divine Presence is in my loins. *(Join hand at the heart)*

I do honor to the God of my own soul

Shining spirit of my spirit

Font of Wisdom

Spring of Love

Source of Power

I offer to you the worship due to every God

(Open hands wide)

Honor to the holy being that is the Center of my Self

Shine bright and flow deep in me, I pray!

Meditate in this space as long as you wish, seeking the vision and voice of the Da Fein as it may show itself to you.

The Nineteen Working
Text With Guidance

In this summary of the work, we present the entire pattern of the meditation with all of its instructions and visualizations. Those who wish may work the rite straight through, but each section has already been presented separately in the instructional chapters of the book. Just following this section we present the text of the Charms only, offered in a decorative and enlarged font, to allow for easier experimentation as you become more familiar with the meditative patterns. Of course the best practice would be to memorize the entire pattern, but that can come with time, as one experiments with the written text.

The Nineteen Working
Stage 1: Shrine Blessing and Open Meditation.

This first section can always serve as a fall-back, or minimum practice. It can be done daily, even as you add additional work during retreats or more focused workings.

The Druid seats himself in her seat, facing east if possible. If there can be hallowed Fire and Water, so much the better. The body should be kept balanced and alert, while relaxed.

Begin your breathing pattern. Find your peace, perhaps using the Bone, Breath and Blood method.

Bless the Water and Fire, as you say:

The Fire, the Well, the Sacred Tree
Flow and Flame and Grow in me
In Land, Sea and Sky, Below and on High,
Let the Water be blessed and the Fire be hallowed.

When you are ready, dip your hand in the Water and sprinkle or lave yourself, then pass your hands through the incense or Fire and bring it onto yourself, as you say:

By the Might of the Waters and the Light of the Fire
Cleansed of ill and bane am I
By the Might of the Waters and the Light of the Fire
Blessed in Land and Sea and Sky

As you cleanse and bless yourself, feel the Water and Fire washing and searing away all that's not in your true pattern of being.

Light an additional offering of incense, and open your heart in welcome to all the Holy Beings. Say:

Gods and Dead and Mighty Sidhe
Powers of Earth and Sky and Sea
By Fire and Well, by Sacred Tree
Welcome I do give to ye.

At this time you may wish to pause in open meditation for as long as you wish. In daily practice it can be enough to do the simple cleansing, followed by open meditation. If you are working a short daily meditation you will go directly from this point to the Closing charm.

Stage 2: Two Powers, Three Realms, Four Airts

The Druid should have a ready skill in the Two Powers, though perhaps somewhat dependent on a lengthy 'induction'. In this exercise we intend to move toward bringing the Two into the self smoothly and quickly, driven by a very simple charm. The second portion of this charm involves centering the self in the Middle World, using the Three Realms and the Four Airts. The accompanying meditation can be developed over time. The Druid should begin where she can, and plan to improve her effects with time and effort.

Resume your center and bring the Two Powers into yourself, swiftly allowing the Waters to rise, followed by the descent of the Light, as you do the Kindling Charm:

Cross your hands on your chest and say:

Powers of the Earth and Sky
Rooted deep and crowned high

Place fingers on forehead, chest and loins in turn, bringing the Two Powers smoothly into each, saying

Flow and kindle in my head
Flow and kindle in my heart
Flow and kindle in my loins

Cross your hands on your chest, feeling the balanced flow of the Two, and say:

Flow and shine in every part.

Remain with hands crossed on the chest or, if you prefer, extend your arms straight from your shoulders. Open yourself to the horizontal plane, to the Three Realms of the world, to the Four Provinces of human power.

The Land upholds me, the Sea surrounds me, the Sky above me.
Before me bounty, behind me wisdom
On my right hand magic, on my left hand strength

Cross hands again on the chest

For the Cauldron is in me.
And I am seated in the Center of Worlds.

At this time you may wish to pause in a meditation in which you compose yourself seating in the center of the Worlds and Realms, with all the Powers at your hand. This meditation can be maintained as long as you wish, simply experiencing the feel of the Pattern of the Worlds around you, with the Fire and Water in you.

Stage 3: The Three Cauldrons
The Two Powers are settled into a clear flow in the self, and the Druid begins to focus them into the Three Cauldrons Attunement:
With the Two Powers established in your body, establish the Three Cauldrons, beginning with your loins.

Envision the Cauldron of Warming low in your belly, see it made of iron, or stone heated by the fire below. Intone the name:
Goriath (goh ree ah)
Envision the combined Light and Shadow flowing into your Cauldron of Warming. As it does, open your awareness to your body. Become aware of your flesh and bone, blood and belly and brain, seeking an awareness of your health and wholeness, and, by will, seeing yourself as hale and well in every part.

Envision the Cauldron of Vocation in the heart. See it made of silver and gold, heated be the fire in your heart. Intone the name:
Ernmas (air'n mahs)
Let the Powers flow into the Cauldron of Movement, and feel your awareness open to your daily life and work. Become aware of your place in the world, among kin and folk and the wide world. From the center that is the Cauldron see the webs of relationship and mutuality that hold your life together. See them made strong, whole and helpful.

Envision the Cauldron of Wisdom in your head. See it made of crystal and amber, lit and warmed by the fire above. Intone the name:
Sofhis (so wish)
Let the Two Powers flow into the Cauldron of Wisdom, and open your spirit to your spiritual way and work. As the Fire and Water fill the Cauldron open your mind to the sources of divine awareness in your life. Feel your Allies draw close, and the Divine In You shine and flow, filling you with the Mead of Inspiration.

As you wish, and as you are able, let your mind rest in balance between these three Cauldrons. Broaden your attention to allow the three sets of images to flow and intertwine. In this weaving there may be things to be learned. Understand that these Cauldrons are always in you, always turned or turning, just as the Two Powers always flow in you. Rest and work in this state as long as you like.

Stage 4: The Elements

Bring the Powers into balance again in yourself, remembering your detachment, remembering your lessons, gently and firmly bringing the Two Powers and the Three Cauldrons into a balanced flow. Remember the vision of the Worlds, and become aware of your flesh as well as you spirit as you work the Duile Attunement.

By the following charm you will turn your attention to the elements of the Worlds, one element at a time. As you are learning the exercise feel free to take each section as slowly as you like, meditating on the union, the co-substance, of your individual existence with the much greater world of All That Is.

**Today I open myself
To the Elements of the World.**

The first triad concerns the Land. Feel your solid flesh sharing its substance with the stones and roots and growing things of the Land, letting it become you, and you, it.

**Eternal stone my bones.
My flesh the warm soil,
My hair the green bounty,**

The second triad concerns the Sea. Feel the processes of your material life as interchangeable with the great ebbs and flows of the endless deep, letting it become you, and you, it.

**The sea my blood,
My breath the wind,
Cool moonlight my mind,**

The third triad concerns the Sky. Feel your reason and emotion and spirit shining and turning among your thoughts, like the eternal heavens. Let it become you, and you, it.

**The sun my face,
My thoughts the clouds,
The stars behind my eyes.**

Feel yourself vanishing into the world, and the world vanishing into you, but all the while, your core of Fire and Water, your Three Cauldrons, remain balanced and firm, even as your awareness opens.

All the world is in me,
And I am in the world.

Stage 5: An Da Fein

If you are able to master your mind again, you may be able to bring all this to a balanced and ordered pattern in yourself. Use your detachment to prevent the awe of the work from overwhelming your will, and find, once again, your center. It is from this Center of All That Is that you can seek the Da Fein — the God of You. The Da Fein is a subtle concept, with many layers of symbolism. You can begin, in this simple exercise, with the symbols of the Light Above and the Light Below, or the falling of the Gold and Silver Drops of the Cauldron of Inspiration. In this symbol we seek the Druids' Treasure, the Celtic version of the Holy Grail, or the Philosopher's Stone, that perfects and empowers and illuminates.

So, seated in balance in the Center of the Worlds, turn your attention to the point just above your nose, a point in a triangle with your two eyes. Turn your awareness into that point, as if it were a doorway, in toward the Center of the Center. Recite the charm as you contemplate the symbols it offers:

I am a kinsman of the Fire
I am a child of the Waters
My flesh is holy, born of the holy union
My Spirit is a drop of the Cauldron of Wonder,
A spark of the Divine Fire.
(Place a hand on the forehead)
The Divine Presence is in my head
(Place hand on heart)
The Divine Presence is in my heart
(Place hand on the loins)
The Divine Presence is in my loins.
(Join hand at the heart)
I do honor to the God of my own soul
Shining spirit of my spirit
Font of Wisdom
Spring of Love
Source of Power

I offer to you the worship due to every God
(Open hands wide)
Honor to the holy being that is the Center of my Self
Shine bright and flow deep in me, I pray!

Meditate in this space as long as you wish, seeking the vision and voice of the Da Fein as it may show itself to you.

Stage 6: Completing

When your meditative practice is complete, take time to return your awareness fully and completely to your body and material senses. Even as you remember what you may have gained or learned in a working, allow your awareness to return to common life and breath. Before you rise from your seat pause for a moment and return to your center in peace. Cross your hands on your chest and say:

The blessings of the Holy Ones be on me and mine
My blessings on all beings,
with peace on thee and thine
The Fire, the Well, the Sacred Tree
Flow and Flame and Grow in me
Thus do I remember the work of the Wise.

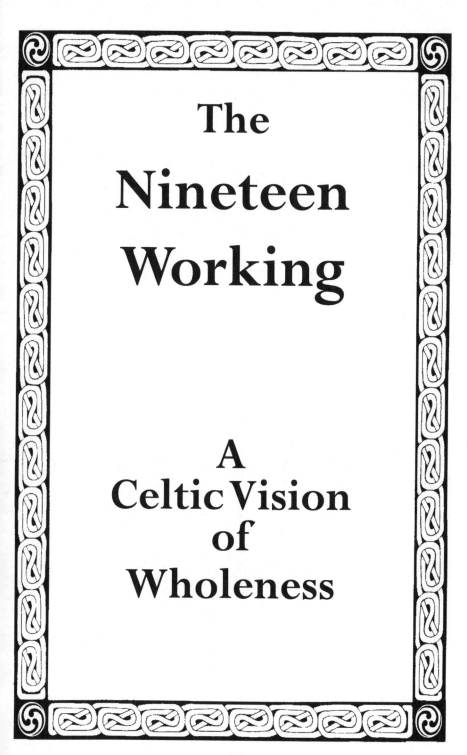

The
Nineteen
Working

A
Celtic Vision
of
Wholeness

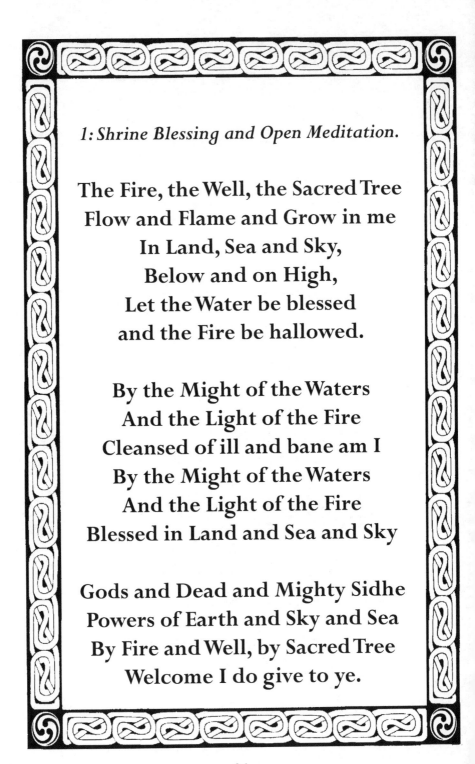

1: Shrine Blessing and Open Meditation.

The Fire, the Well, the Sacred Tree
Flow and Flame and Grow in me
In Land, Sea and Sky,
Below and on High,
Let the Water be blessed
and the Fire be hallowed.

By the Might of the Waters
And the Light of the Fire
Cleansed of ill and bane am I
By the Might of the Waters
And the Light of the Fire
Blessed in Land and Sea and Sky

Gods and Dead and Mighty Sidhe
Powers of Earth and Sky and Sea
By Fire and Well, by Sacred Tree
Welcome I do give to ye.

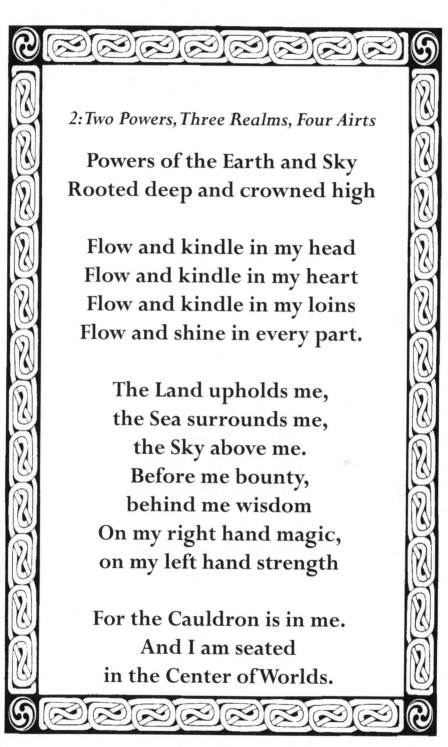

2: Two Powers, Three Realms, Four Airts

Powers of the Earth and Sky
Rooted deep and crowned high

Flow and kindle in my head
Flow and kindle in my heart
Flow and kindle in my loins
Flow and shine in every part.

The Land upholds me,
the Sea surrounds me,
the Sky above me.
Before me bounty,
behind me wisdom
On my right hand magic,
on my left hand strength

For the Cauldron is in me.
And I am seated
in the Center of Worlds.

3: The Three Cauldrons

Goriath (goh ree ah)

Ernmas (air'n mahs)

Sofhis (so wish)

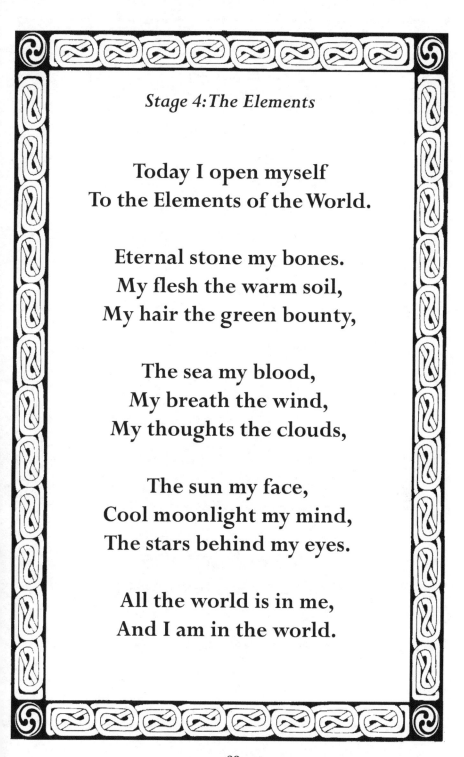

Stage 4: The Elements

Today I open myself
To the Elements of the World.

Eternal stone my bones.
My flesh the warm soil,
My hair the green bounty,

The sea my blood,
My breath the wind,
My thoughts the clouds,

The sun my face,
Cool moonlight my mind,
The stars behind my eyes.

All the world is in me,
And I am in the world.

5: *An Da Fein*

I am a kinsman of the Fire
I am a child of the Waters
My flesh is holy,
born of the holy union
My Spirit is a drop
of the Cauldron of Wonder,
A spark of the Divine Fire.
The Divine Presence is in my head
The Divine Presence is in my heart
The Divine Presence is in my loins.
I do honor to the God
of my own soul
Shining spirit of my spirit
Font of Wisdom
Spring of Love
Source of Power
I offer to you the worship
due to every God
Honor to the holy being
that is the Center of my Self
Shine bright and flow deep in me,
I pray!

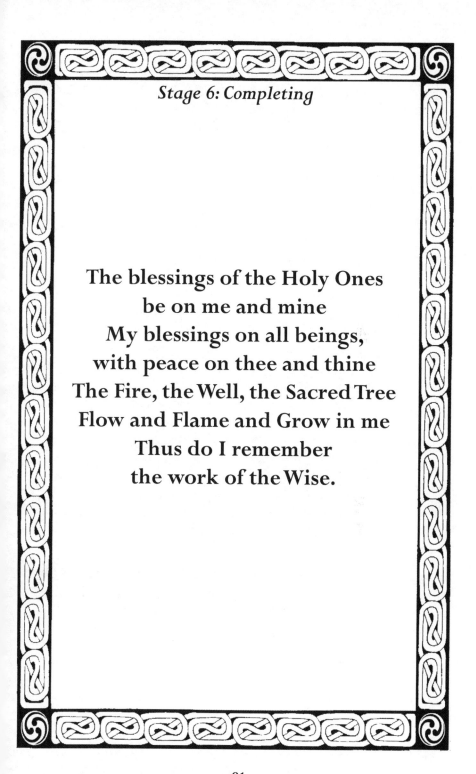

Stage 6: Completing

The blessings of the Holy Ones
be on me and mine
My blessings on all beings,
with peace on thee and thine
The Fire, the Well, the Sacred Tree
Flow and Flame and Grow in me
Thus do I remember
the work of the Wise.

The
Fourth Cycle

Trance Vision
&
The Inner Grove

The Fourth Cycle - The Road to the Spirit World

Our first three cycles were concerned with the Druid's own mind and spirit, with calming the chattering mind, ordering and empowering the self and with the vision of the Sacred Cosmos. These practices will train the faculties of concentration, visualization and relaxation, and will also strengthen the Druid's heart and mind. All of this contributes to the work of spirit-vision that is taught in the next cycles.

In the realm of modern magic one of the most notable new trends in the last 150 years is the importance of the willed production of visions. Perhaps electric lights have dazzled our inner sight, or multiple bright and perfect color images made imagination trivial. We live in an age when the contents of the mind may seem pale and unreal compared to the constructs of popular entertainment. But in the work of magic there is nothing trivial about the imagination. The imagination is both the perceptual equipment and the tool of construction that allow us to work in the realm of vision that is the dwelling-place of spirits.

The techniques given here are a bridge between the 19th and early twentieth-century practice of 'guided visualization' and the late twentieth-century adaptation of so-called 'shamanic' technique. They employ guided imagery as a starting point for further self-guided vision-travel. Essentially the magician enters a kind of waking dream, in which the personal will has some directing power but in which the landscapes and events are largely outside the control of that will.

In this vision-trance the personal mind comes nearer to the transpersonal reality of the Otherworld, the real home of the spirits, and the ground in which inner energies flow. The spirits can speak to us inside these states much more directly than to our distracted common awareness, and our perceptions of the inner powers and realities of things are sharpened.

This cycle also works with the classic magical technique of the Inner Temple. In many world ritual traditions it is common for adepts to create envisioned working spaces that parallel their material temples. In these Inner Groves and Temples we can create beauty that is beyond our material means, and into these places we can call the Gods and spirits in a much more direct fashion. While vision work does not depend on the creation of an Inner temple, there are many advantages to doing this traditional work.

This instruction does not pay a great deal of attention to ritual. It does, however, assume that the student is able to work basic ritual and is doing so during the learning of these techniques. As always, the techniques are based in Pagan Druidic symbolism and ritual forms, but are easily adapted for other systems.

The Threshold of the Otherworld:
Part 1 – Concepts of the Other

Throughout Celtic story we find humans meeting the spirits in ways and places outside of or beyond common life. Gods, messengers, allies and opponents arrive among mortals bringing tales of their homes, of strange halls and wild places both near and far. In turn the tales tell of mortals who visit Other Folk. It is from these tales that we begin to understand the nature of what we often simply call the Otherworld.

The tales describe the dwellings of the Other Clans as being both very near to our mortal world and very far from our common lands. The armies of the Sidhe ride out from beneath the land. Mortals enter the courts and feasts of the Lords of the Mound, leaving behind common time and place. Other tales tell of emissaries arriving from over the sea, or of mortals who voyage, and of the lands of wonder, danger and vision that lie beyond the ocean wave.

From the tales we can construct several images of the Other Worlds of Gaelic story. Some tales tell of the Land Over the Waves, a place of eternal youth and delight, of beauty and music. Others show us strange feasting halls and palaces, often located beneath the mounds of the land. In some stories mortals pass through mists to find themselves in a kind of parallel forest where strange beasts and the Noble Ones ride. In such Other Lands are found the fortresses and halls of the people of the Mound – the Daoine Sidhe.

Your studies should offer plenty of chances to read these tales. It is useful to immerse your imagination in the motifs of Celtic story. These provide raw materials with which we can build an understanding of the Celtic Otherworld.

It may be that the ancient idea of the Otherworld bears a resemblance to various metaphysical models. Those familiar with western magical systems might compare the Otherworld with the 'astral plane' or the 'etheric realm'. However, the Celtic spirit-lands don't seem to be causal to the common world in the way the 'astral' is sometimes described to be. We might find a parallel with the Dreamtime of the Australian First Peoples – a mythic, storied and ritual reality in which mortals participate along with the Gods and spirits. Hindu cosmology presents a variety of 'lokas' – worlds – in which Gods, spirits, ancestors and daemons dwell. The Norse have a similar system of Nine Realms. Celtic lore is far less specific about the number and order of the realms or worlds, though a variety of environments

95

are described.

Modern Pagan metaphysics brings additional popular models. Cosmological elements from Asian shamanism have made their way into much of Neopaganism, though it is fair to say that they may have done the same thing in ancient days. The basic map of Underworld, Midrealm and Heavens has become important in Our Druidry and we will use that triad in this Initiate's work, as well.

There is also a scientific or rational approach that may have some value. A good deal of research has been done into 'altered states of awareness' – states of perception and cognition that have always been connected with 'religious' or 'spiritual' events. Scientists have begun to identify the brain-wave patterns that correspond to events such as trance-vision or mystical awareness. This may include what some call 'paranormal' or 'ESP' effects. While it possible to develop an entire model of magical art from such ideas we will give it little attention here, preferring a more mythic approach.

Part 2 – Vision and the Threshold

One of the primary spiritual powers of Druidry is the Power of Seeing. In the later folklore of the Gaels we hear of an da sheiliagh – the double-sight or second sight. That sort of seeing is commonly used to discern worldly events, but there are also tales of the ability to see the Other Folk, their halls and lands and works.

This traditional second sight is sometimes a gift at birth but can also be gained as a gift from the Noble Ones, or through deliberate magical work. We'll discuss some folkloric means of gaining the Other Sight but for the most part we will use other approaches. We will focus on the use of will and imagination to create states that can allow us to 'step through' into Other places.

In this month's first exercises we will enter an imagined series of landscapes and environments. In some cases we will consciously select or design the spaces. In others we will enter visions that we do not deliberately create. We will consider this half-constructed, half-discovered imaginal world to be a Threshold, a place Between the common world and the independent reality of the Other Places. We can move our point of view, our 'presence', into this Threshold realm in a form we invent, and in the same way the Gods and spirits can create forms that move and live in that space. The forms we see (and make) in the Threshold may or may not be the 'true' forms of the spirits but that need not prevent us from speaking to them through those forms. The Threshold is a reflection both of our common world and of the Other realms beyond.

Like all intelligent beings we have the Power of Shaping as well as of Seeing. Our ability to craft mental images has a reality in the Inner Realms as surely as the work of our hands in the common world. Just as the Gods and spirits create their Other spaces around them, so we can make small spaces, shaped by will and vision. Obviously we modern students have only small skill or power as we begin. We start by gathering the powers of Earth and Sky – they respond to our shaping by taking on form as we will. With those materials we can shape as we will in the world of vision. A large measure of our practice in this system will be devoted these techniques, and their results.

While we may consciously shape and influence it, the Threshold realm exists without our conscious making. Just as the landscapes of dream occur as if subjectively real so the places of Threshold are waiting for us when we arrive. Just as in a lucid dream we can shape events and places, but the life of the Threshold realm goes on, even around our conscious constructions.

Part 3 – First Steps in the Mist

There are many traditional methods of moving awareness from the common toward the Other. All of them are methods of moving your personal point-of-view away from your physical location and into the Threshold realm of vision. Fasting, secret herbs, drum and dance, austerity and pain have all been used to free the mind from its common boundaries. We will depend on a gentler method based on concentration and visualization.

The very first Threshold technique is to learn to rise and move within an imagined point-of-view. In some spiritual systems students are taught to develop a detailed, repeating and specific 'body of vision' which serves as the seer's 'vehicle'. This does have value, but we find it best to recommend a more natural approach. Each of us carries a basic self-image and it is in that form that we can most easily approach our vision journeys.

One important trick of basic journey-work is to train yourself to keep your point-of-view located 'behind the eyes' of your vision-self. It is worthwhile, as an exercise, to pay attention to the physical reality of walking in your body. The walking meditation taught in the ADF Dedicant's Nature Awareness work offers a chance to contemplate the sensory reality of seeing the world through the screen of your eyes. It is then possible to use memory to inform your visions. By learning to keep your point of view firmly fixed in one place and in one direction at a time you create a sense of reality in your early visions that helps you move into the Threshold realm. Your point of view may move by drifting, flying or purposeful striding but you should be careful to keep it in one place at a time in most cases.

Our first exercise uses memory and visualization to introduce the technique of moving and seeing in vision. Entering basic trance you will imagine that you have opened your eyes, right where you sit in your ritual space. From there you will experiment with standing in your point-of-view and exploring the familiar environment of your Shrine, remembering the details and visualizing them clearly while holding your perception behind your vision-eyes.

From that beginning you can move deeper into the Threshold in a variety of ways. There are many classic methods of deepening through visualization – descending stairs, drifting down through water, etc. We will use a symbol drawn directly from Celtic story – the Mist of the Between. By passing through the vision of the thick mist so common in the ancient forests you can emerge much deeper within the Threshold realm.

We will use the Mist-passing as a means to move from the simple memory-based initial exercises to a more spontaneous and unconstructed locale. While we will use signposts to attempt to reach specific destination the first efforts at passing the Mist may always produce surprises. In order to make the early experiments more orderly we will focus on a familiar goal – the Inner Nemeton.

In the first technique you will begin by 'rising' from your seated form to stand in the vision of your ritual space. You may more clearly perceive spiritual presences in this space, but you remain very close to the common world. By passing the Mist we seek to enter a space in which we can both discover and create a greater, more ideal Sacred Grove. In the next technique you will move on to the work of passing the Mist and beginning the Inner Grove. This will become a base of operations for many further visions and workings.

Rising in Vision

Our work begins with the skill of moving your point-of-view in envisioned environments. You should work this exercise before your Shrine, or with your portable Hallows outdoors. It may have more value if worked at a Home Shrine to which you have already committed some effort.

Let the Druid be seated at the Shrine, with all required.

Opening:

• *Work the Bone, Breath and Blood, and the Kindling Charm, or Two Powers centering.*

• *Light the Fire and silver the Water, saying:*

Fire I kindle, Water I pour
The Hearth and Well I hallow.
By the Mother of the Land be hallowed
By the Lord of Wisdom be hallowed.
Blessed and made sacred to the work,
Beneath the Tree of the Worlds.

Sprinkle and cense yourself and all as you say:

So by the Might of the Water and the Light of the Fire
Let this place be cleansed of all ill,
Made whole and holy
For the Work of the Wise.

Simple offerings are made, either of grain into a real fire, or incense into a censer, saying:

I make offering to the Earth Mother
Bless me in my work
I make offering to the Lord of Wisdom
Open the Ways for me
I make offering to the Dead,
To the Spirits, to the Shining Gods.
Bless me in my work
With Wisdom, Love and Power.

The Working:
• *Seat yourself comfortably upright, back straight.*

•*Work a short blessing of the space, or the full Grove opening and Gate if you wish - in your first exercises it might be best to work the full opening, with the Gate.*

• *Renew and strengthen your Earth and Heavens contacts.*

• *Feel the cool Earth Power and the hot Sky Power meet in your head, meet in your heart, and meet in your loins.*

• *And from the meeting-places, feel the mingling of the Powers flow out into your whole form — into your hands, into your form, into your eyes. Where you have eyes of flesh, so you now have eyes of vision.*

• *Open your eyes of vision, and use your memory of the setting of your Shrine and tools. As you remember them, envision them, so that it is as if you see them with open eyes. It is the eyes of vision that open in this way, and it is in the eyes of vision that you will move.*

•*With your material eyes closed, decide to stand in your vision form. Allow your eyes to rise, effortlessly. You rise to your natural height, and take a moment to gaze upon your Shrine and Hallows as if you had stood in flesh. Allow the details of your Shrine to become clear.*

• *This is the threshold of the Threshold. You are in the material world, seeing it only with your vision's eye. Move around your Shrine a bit; allow your point of view to see the Shrine from different angles. If you are in a place you know well you might move around further, using memory to help your vision be built true.*

•*You may, if you wish, look down at yourself, though there is no need... you feel the presence of your hands... of your body upright... in the presence of the Hallows.*

•*Allow the natural setting to resolve into greater detail... gaze around the perimeter of your clearing or room, seeking details... gaze all around...*

•*Widen your vision, and behold all that you have beheld... remember... remember the forms that you have seen, the locale you have been in...for it is by memory that you will return...*

• *So, standing before the vision of your Shrine, remember your body... allow your point of view to return to where your body is seated... you may see yourself seated there... turn and face the Shrine, and allow your point of view to descend, sitting down into your material form... settling again into your flesh... bringing your eyes to eyes, heart to heart, loins to loins... breathing deep...*

• *Allow yourself to return for a moment to your basic peace... sitting calmly in yourself... then stretch... open your eyes... and be present again before your Fire...*

• *Close your Gate and the work as usual.*

Closing:

• *Upon concluding you should thank any beings who have aided you, and end formally:*

Let bound be bound and wound be wound
Thus all is done, and done, and well done
And thus I end what was begun.
To the Three Holy Kindreds I give thanks
To the Lord of Wisdom I give thanks
To the Mother of All I give thanks
Thus do I remember the work of the wise.

The Inner Grove

The skills of seership, of perceiving and moving in the Otherworlds, are seated in the human imagination. In our age, it is common to think of the imagination as an entirely subjective and personal faculty. Western science has been so successful at manipulating the material world that many have come to believe only in material causes and effects. To the ancients the human mind was understood as a part of the spiritual world. The spiritual world was understood as being in a relationship of mutual causation with the material. What happens in the material world affects the spiritual, and what happens in the spiritual affects the material. This spiritual world is the Celtic Otherworld, so famed in the tales. The Otherworld is the place where stories live, where the Gods and Goddesses move, where the Dead have their halls. It is always near us, yet heroes reach it in far voyages. The human imagination functions as our spiritual organ of Otherworld perception, as our on-board tool set with which we shape the Otherworld.

The methods of vision which we'll use in this work begin with the imagination. Using our powers of vision and shaping we will begin by constructing interior events and landscapes. We may assume that such constructs are at first entirely internal and subjective. However, every mind is connected with the All-Mind, rooted in the Waters, crowned at the Pole Star. These events and scenes that we create for ourselves are like temples that we build in a forest. There we do our work, make our offerings, and wait to see what answers come to us from the depths of the trackless wild.

The spaces we make in our minds are conceived of as connected with every other mind and with the All-Mind by the currents and eddies of the Deep Waters, by the reflections of the Light. When we have made our inner landscapes well, they become paths by which the mental and spiritual reality of beings other than ourselves can reach us. Just as the deer and birds might emerge from the forest around a temple, so the Gods and Spirits come to the edge of our vision. When this happens, what had been a purely internal and subjective experience begins to show signs of influences from outside the personal mind. New ideas, insights and inspirations become available as the personal spirit opens to the greater world.

In the same way, we can use deliberately constructed environments as a launching-point for journeys in vision as we send our own spirits out on the currents of the Otherworld. These spirit-voyages take us away from our carefully constructed inner locales, out into uncharted places. While these visions may begin, once again, as efforts of willed imagination, they are also able to lead us outside our common mind toward realms of the transpersonal.

So we begin with deliberate construction of vision and seek to use these constructs as tools of communication with the Gods and Spirits. We will take as one of our primary mechanisms of entrancement and journeying the image of the Wizard's Mist.

Techniques of Trance Vision

Having begun with some basic trance-vision techniques, your task now is to learn to easily bring yourself into the Inner Grove. In our first exercises we used a detailed trance script to enter the Mist and emerge into the Grove. In the next we will begin there again, but will then use spoken-word and vision-keys to allow you to quickly enter trance, pass the Mist and arrive on the Threshold of the Otherworld.

It will be useful to learn to make the transition to the Inner Grove easily and quickly. You will find many applications for this traditional magical technique, and you should lay the foundation well at this phase of your work. As always regular practice is the only reliable method of gaining skill.
As in all these early stages you will benefit from practicing the techniques at least three time per week. The weekly retreat days are you opportunities to learn the basic forms through the exercises given here. In further practice you should work to integrate the technique, either repeating the exercises or working in your own way. The later exercises in this program will be enhanced by good skill in entering and working in the Inner Grove

Working with Scripts and Outlines

This program of training has several central goals. Through the exercises and rites in this program (especially when combined with the ritual work of the Book of Summoning) we hope to build skills in spirit-journeying as well as in the Inner Sight that allows us to see the spirits and energies that imbue our work. The trancework intends to make awareness in the Threshold state second nature. In later techniques you will learn the Double-Sight, in which you work both in the Threshold and in the common world. In order to reach that level of skill you will begin with trances based on scripts, but you must move past them, to self-directed and free-form vision.

Learning to navigate the Inner can be much like learning any complex new landscape. First you might use detailed maps (even spoken-voice navigators) to find basic destinations. Soon you will need maps or written notes only to locate new or unusual destinations. In time you learn to find your own short-cuts.

In this training we begin with fully scripted guided visualizations. These scripts are the result of long experiment and will reliably bring you to the desired interior places. In order to use them well it is best to hear them actually spoken aloud. Recordings of many are available, but there is value in recording your own voice reading the scripts. If you have a fellow student or partner who understands your work you might also be able to have them read for you, perhaps taking turns being reader and visionary.

If none of those options are available then you might try working the visualizations while you read them. This might be useful in a kind of 'dress-rehearsal' way. By reading through the images, and making an effort to 'send a vision' while you read you can perhaps 'pre-plan' the journey and take a step toward independent work. Once you have practiced a technique this way several times you should be able to work it in detail in an eyes-closed, fully visualized trance. In any such trance the goal is to generate a full, quasi-sensory experience. This is nearly impossible for modern people to do while using the physical senses in reading or speaking. A full trance will produce a much more effective experience.

The next level of skill is to be able to work from memorized outlines. Each of our full scripts can be reduced to an outline, a simple sequence that reminds you of the details of trances and locales already familiar. Remembering the order of the steps of a trance tends to produce a clearer memory of the detail of the transitions between the steps. We will discuss the creation of markers and symbolic sequences, and provide short outlines for each of the trance patterns ahead.

Defining a Path

The Inner Grove technique involves the establishment of a Threshold locale based upon a reflection of your specific Hallows and personal ritual space. We can conceive of this Threshold Grove as "nearby' our material locale, and the path between them as a short one. Still it is important to have a clear set of symbols to define the way.

As we set out to learn to navigate the Otherworld we find ourselves in a journey of exploration with only the vaguest of maps. We step into the Mist with little beyond our will and vision to guide us. As we each establish our own route through the Mist we must create guides and markers to show us the way.

Creating a "path" through the Mist is a matter of using symbols and memory to lead our awareness reliably to the same state or locale each time we wish to visit it. We create a set of "signposts" that allow us to focus the trance state accurately. This allows us to build Threshold locales that we can revisit, improve and use in practical ways.

The first signposts on the road to the Inner Grove are the very tools of your own material nemeton or shrine. Your own Fire, Well and Tree are talismans of the Other, each one a direct manifestation of the Otherworld Powers, and their image is the first symbol through which you will pass. We will use the vision of the combining of the Fire and Water in the Hallows to generate the Mist. So we will begin by focusing on reality as we find it – the real presence of the Fire and water – and proceed to an initial visualization of the Mist of the Between.

Throughout these lessons we will use the Mist of the Between as our primary symbol of the transition between worlds. The featureless, engulfing Mist is the ever-present Boundary, as close as our own ability to perceive it. The Mist is, however, pathless and without landmarks. Crossing the Mist is a matter of a firm will that keeps you moving forward, and of creating your own road-signs and gates.

We call the Mist by finding the place of Between in the combination of Fire and Water in the Grove. The combination of symbols in the Hallows creates a Sacred Center, and a Boundary Between, by being a place of neither-nor-and-both. In that place the Mist is always available, and we can enter through the images of our Hallows into the edge of Threshold. In order to arrive quickly and reliably in the same place it is useful to create a sigil that is always used to grant admission to the locale. For this you might use the Gate-Sign, as given here, with any symbol proper to you and your Inner Grove in the center of it. The basic Dedicant Druid sigil might be used if you like something universal, representing the Fire and Water in the Grove. It is best to choose a simple symbol, perhaps one that can be actually sketched with a finger or wand. This figure is then envisioned or drawn in the Mist. By passing through that symbol in vision you will emerge into your Inner Grove.

So that is our simple path to what will become a familiar place. We begin in our Middle World, then pass through the Fire and Water into the Mist. We formulate the Gate Sign in the Mist, and pass through it into the Inner Grove.

Through regular practice this can become a short and easy road. In one smooth transition you will move past the Fire and Water through the Mist and the Sign into the Grove. In our effort to craft techniques based on old Druidic forms you might choose to use a simple spoken (or sung) charm. In time the recitation of the charm alone will seem to accomplish the transition.

Working in the Grove

Your first work in the Grove is to enhance and complete the details of its setting and structure. Upon your first arrival you will have had some basic perceptions.. Perhaps you had misty glimpses or perhaps a detailed vision appeared. In any case the task before you is to develop those basics into a detailed environment of your own Inner Grove.

Your Threshold locale should be built carefully. Your initial goal is consistency. Any additions or changes that you make in the Grove should be permanent, unless you consciously change them. Each time that you arrive you should expect to see any work which you have done previously. You should employ a firm memory and will to build your Grove as a lasting artifact.

The style and form of the permanent Hallows in your Grove or Shrine is you own choice, though you will probably find some basic forms and materials in place on arrival. You will find the primary reflections of your own altar of Fire, your Well, and a live Tree or fine pillar. These will be arranged in the same pattern as your material Hallows. In your Threshold Grove you can choose to make them monumental or intimate, ornate or simple. Those choices are strictly personal and strictly aesthetic. What matters is that you are able to accurately reproduce the vision each time that you arrive. While you are looking for conscious and deliberate creation, don't forget to consider including ways in which you might be able to find unexpected detail when you look closely.

Some traditions instruct us to visualize and experience the whole process of building the Hallows as though we were doing it materially. You might dig the Well or construct the Fire Altar from brick or stone. Even if you choose to simply shape the Threshold by your will and vision it is worthwhile to include some of this sort of effort. The creation of tactile and experiential memories is an excellent way to make your Grove live for you.

Choosing the form of the elements of the Grove provides an opportunity to research historic and cultural ritual and temple forms. You can study what traditional sacred wells look like. Do you want a Fire Altar built upon the ground, or a sacred vessel, a brazier or cauldron? Should it be round or square? Look for images of ancient sacred pillars and columns, and consider what symbols you would use. Would you prefer a living sacred tree as the center of your Grove? In your visits during this moon you will choose and create the forms of your Grove.

The first stage of completion of the Inner Grove requires only a well-realized natural setting with the Three Hallows set within it. Taking your time and effort to create it is a key work of learning the Nine Moons magic. Once the Grove is established you will begin to use it to work ritual, to seek deeper meditation and to serve as a starting-point for journeying.

Passing the Mist & the Vision of the Hallows.

The work will allow the discovery or creation of an Inner working space - a visionary locale from which journeys may be begun, and into which the spirits will be called. There are many such methods, but here we give one that is based on seeking the Inner counterpart to the material locales we create for ritual.

Opening:
•*Work the Kindling Charm, or Two Powers centering.*
• *Light the Fire and silver the Water, saying:*

Fire I kindle, Water I pour
The Hearth and Well I hallow.
By the Mother of the Land be hallowed
By the Lord of Wisdom be hallowed.
Blessed and made sacred to the work,
Beneath the Tree of the Worlds.

Sprinkle and cense yourself and all as you say:

So by the Might of the Water and the Light of the Fire
Let this place be cleansed of all ill,
Made whole and holy
For the Work of the Wise.

Simple offerings are made, either of grain into a real fire, or incense into a censer, saying:

I make offering to the Earth Mother
Bless me in my work
I make offering to the Lord of Wisdom
Open the Ways for me
I make offering to the Dead,
To the Spirits, to the Shining Gods.
Bless me in my work
With Wisdom, Love and Power.

•*At this point the details of the work at hand are performed.*

The Working:

- Establish primary circulation of the Two Powers, perhaps using the Kindling Charm.

- Feel the cool Earth Power and the hot Sky Power meet in your head, meet in your heart, and meet in your loins.

- And in the meeting-places, feel the mingling of the Powers begin to produce the Mist - the streams of vapor pouring out of your Inner Cauldrons, flowing out from the roots of the Tree, where Fire and Water meet.

- visualize the Mist gathering and thickening, beginning to accumulate. Even as the Powers are meeting in your own body, and the Mist flows from you, you may perceive the Mist approaching from around you, from the Gates in your Nemeton.

- The Mist gathers, growing thicker, and collecting around your feet... around your hips and loins... around your arms and chest. It grows thick and opaque, and rises, at last, to surround your head.

-With your eyes closed, envision the Wizard's Mist as it surrounds you... See it grey and silver and white, sometimes glistening, sometimes shadowed... growing thicker, warm and comforting.

- This is the Mist of the Between... the place of neither/nor... neither waking nor sleeping, neither in the common world or in the Otherworld... a place where journeying may happen... a place of unknown possibility... rest here for a while... rest in meditation as your mind holds the presence of the swirling Mist of the Border...

- Now, seated in the Mist, it is time to begin... in your imagination's eye... in your Inner Vision... not with your physical body... Stand up... Use your body in vision... brace yourself... and rise up from where you are seated... feel your point-of-view rise with your head... holding your point-of-view behind your imagined eyes...You stand up in your vision body... you take a step forward... and stand in the Mist...

- You may, if you wish, look down at yourself, though there is no need... you feel the presence of your hands... of your body upright... as the Mist swirls all around you...

- *Now it is your task to part the Mist and move into the vision reality of your ritual space, upon the land on which you began... bring to mind your goal and your target... let your memory draw it before you... see its shape and color... recall its nature...*

- *In vision, reach your hand before you, and draw a triskel in the Mist before you... focused on your goal image, see the Mist swirl where you draw... and see it begin to part...*

- *Now the Mist begins to thin... as though blown by an unfelt wind... now, with memory and will... you see the scene resolve before you... your goal-image, the Nemeton, revealed in its Otherworld form... elements of the same scene that you left when you called the Mist... see it resolve in your Inner Eye... as the Mist clears around you... revealing the Inner reflection of the common world...*

- *You behold the Inner Grove resolving before you... you see the details more clearly now...*

- *The Inner World is brighter, but perhaps less 'in focus'... it glimmers and wavers, resolving only when you gaze directly at a scene... sometimes resolving sharply, all on its own...*

- *Where you have placed your hallows you may see other forms, Inner forms... a Well... a pillar... the Fire in the Tintean... that Sacred Fire that shines in every world... and the presence of the Gate... the Way Between the Worlds... appearing however it is true and real for you...*

- *In your vision body, turn and look around you... turn to your right... and to your left... turn at last and look behind you... you are aware of your body, seated in the common world... You take note of its position... as you look at the Inner World around you...*

(If this is your first experience of passing the Mists, or if anything doesn't feel right about the experience, this is as far as you should go. Skip to the return instructions.)

- *If all feels well to you, you may wish to walk out into the Inner... For these first experiments, remaining near to your physical body... to the original Inner Grove locale... your Sacred Fire, lit before you, will always be visible to you... always be a beacon for returning... no matter how far you roam…*

- So, for a time, explore the Inner Land in which you find yourself… look at the plants and stones… look round to see the presence of birds, beasts, or beings… but for now, do not seek to interact with them… only observe…

- And, after a time, turn and look for the glint of your Sacred Fire… and return to the place where you can dimly glimpse your body…

The Return

- Standing in vision before your body… turn, and step backward into the space where your body is sitting… raise your spirit-hand before you… and make a tuathal triskel in the air before you… sit down into your body… and see the Mist rise around you… renew your center… feel the Earth and Sky Powers meeting in your flesh… as the Mist rises around you… you are again in the place between…

-Remember your body, and as the mist parts again, breathe deep… feel the air flow in your lungs… the blood course in your veins… open your eyes, and know that your spirit has returned fully to your flesh… stretch… and be finished with the trance.

Closing:

• *Upon concluding you should thank any beings who have aided you, and end formally:*

Let bound be bound and wound be wound
Thus all is done, and done, and well done
And thus I end what was begun.
To the Three Holy Kindreds I give thanks
To the Lord of Wisdom I give thanks
To the Mother of All I give thanks
Thus do I remember the work of the wise.

An Alternate Vision, for Ritual

This series of visions is more directly adapted for working physical ritual while in trance, experiencing the powers and presences of the rite while doing the physical sacrifices, etc.:

- *Feel the cool Earth Power and the hot Sky Power meet in your head, meet in your heart, and meet in your loins.*

- *And in the meeting-places, feel the mingling of the Powers begin to produce the Mist - the streams of vapor pouring out of your Inner Cauldrons, flowing out from the roots of the Tree, where Fire and Water meet.*

- *visualize the Mist gathering and thickening, beginning to accumulate. Even as the Powers are meeting in your own body, and the Mist flows from you, you may also perceive the Mist approaching from around you, from the Gates in your Nemeton.*

- *The Mist gathers, growing thicker, and collecting around your feet... rising around your hips and loins... around your arms and chest. It grows thick and opaque, and rises, at last, to surround your head.*

- *With your eyes closed, envision the Wizard's Mist as it surrounds you... See it grey and silver and white, sometimes glistening, sometimes shadowed... growing thicker, warm and comforting.*

- *This is the Mist of the Between... the place of neither/nor... neither waking nor sleeping, neither in the common world or in the Otherworld... a place where journeying may happen... a place of unknown possibility... rest here for a while... rest in meditation as your mind holds the presence of the swirling Mist of the Border...*

- *Now, seated in the Mist, you may feel yourself begin to drift... your form bobbing and slowly drifting, as if cut loose from the moorings of reality... and for a time, you drift... you feel the presence of your hands... of your body... you watch with your vision eye as the Mist swirls all around you...*

- *As you float in the Mist of the Between, let the image of your own Shrine, it's Fire and Well and Tree, be your target and your goal... see it before you, and feel yourself impelled by its pull... moving in your seat through the mist toward it again...*

- *Now it is your task to part the Mist and move into the vision reality* of your ritual space, upon the land on which you began... bring clearly to mind your goal and your target... your own home shrine or the ritual space that you've established... let your memory draw it before you... see its shape and color... recall its nature...

- Both in vision and in your flesh, reach your hand before you, and draw a spiral in the Mist before you... spiraling outward from the center, turning tuathal... let your vision now be focused on your goal image, see the Mist swirl where you draw... and see it begin to part...

- Now the Mist begins to thin... as though blown by an unfelt wind... now, with memory and will... you see the scene resolve before you... your own Shrine or Nemeton, revealed in its Otherworld form... elements of the same scene that you left when you called the Mist... see it resolve in your Inner Eye... as the Mist clears around you... revealing the Threshold reflection of the common world...

- You behold the Threshold vision of the ritual space resolving around you... details becoming clear...

- The Threshold may be brighter, but perhaps less 'in focus'... it glimmers and wavers, or perhaps retains a misty quality... resolving only when you gaze directly at a scene... sometimes resolving sharply, all on its own...

- Where you have placed your hallows you may see other forms, Inner forms... a well... a pillar... the fire in the altar... that Sacred Fire that shines in every world... and the presence of the Gate... the Way Between the Worlds... appearing however it is true and real for you...

- In your vision body only, turn your head and look around you... turn to your right... and to your left... you are aware of your body, seated in the common world... and you fix your vision-form firmly into your body...

- Hold your two hands, both of vision and of flesh, easily before you, palms up, and let the Fire and Water flow into them... eyes still closed, sit in your power, the Two flowing and shining, gazing in Threshold vision upon your Shrine before you... and when you wish, open your eyes slowly...

- Hold fast to your concentration, and keep the Threshold Vision before your eyes... the material vision becomes clear as well, and you know the Double Sight... your eyes of vision open even as you are free to work...

113

The Charm of the Open Eye

Once you have had success with these experiments, and have a sense of what it means to work ritual while in the Threshold Vision, the process can be reduced to a ritual shorthand that flows well in a ritual magic setting. This method depends entirely on the skill of the mage. Of course it is not the simple performance of the charm and gestures that make it happen, though once you are well-drilled in its use it can come to seem that way.

The Mist Calling

1: Find your basic trance and abide in it for a moment

2: allow the Mist to arise from you and around you

3: close your material eyes for a time, and drift in the Mist

4: envision your goal, and be drawn toward it

5: draw the Opening Spiral with both material and vision-hand

6: Let the Mist be cleared away, and behold the Threshold vision of your Shrine

7: Open your eyes, and know the Double Sight

So this short charm should be recited three times, and then the Short Road will be easily remembered as you go.

Between Fire and Water, I find my balance
From the Union of Fire and Water the Mist rises
Let the Mist carry me, and my Eye of Vision open
Let the Eye lead me, and my vision be clear and true
Let my Vision enchant me, with the sorcerer's sight
Eye of Vision, eye of flesh, let me see clearly
That the Work of the Wise be done.

Three Trances for the Inner Grove

• *Outline of Basic Inner Grove trance-vision:*

1: Basic trance, induced by whatever method you prefer.

2: Rise in Vision, stand up from your body and place yourself behind you Inner Eyes. Behold the Hallows in the common world, through your vision-eyes.

3: Call the Mist to obscure all.

4: Envision the Gate Sign with a personal key-symbol.

5: Hold your goal-will as the Inner Grove, and step through the Gate out of the mist into a Threshold landscape containing the Hallows in the Inner.

6: Remember the Grove and recognize it as you have made it.

7: Recite a Grove Charm at the Inner Fire to establish your presence

8: Do any other works.

9: Return

The Trances:

A Simple Opening and Closing

Let the Druid have her Fire and Well tools, and whatever else she needs for the work at hand.

Opening:

•*Work the Kindling Charm, or Two Powers centering.*

• *Light the Fire and silver the Water, saying:*

Fire I kindle, Water I pour

The Hearth and Well I hallow.

By the Mother of the Land be hallowed

By the Lord of Wisdom be hallowed.

Blessed and made sacred to the work,

Beneath the Tree of the Worlds.

Sprinkle and cense yourself and all as you say:

So by the Might of the Water and the Light of the Fire
Let this place be cleansed of all ill,
Made whole and holy
For the Work of the Wise.

Simple offerings are made, either of grain into a real fire, or incense into a censer, saying:

I make offering to the Earth Mother
Bless me in my work
I make offering to the Lord of Wisdom
Open the Ways for me
I make offering to the Dead,
To the Spirits, to the Shining Gods.
Bless me in my work
With Wisdom, Love and Power.

• *At this point the details of the trance at hand are performed, per the scripts below.*

Closing:

• *Upon concluding you should thank any beings who have aided you, and end formally:*

Let bound be bound and wound be wound
Thus all is done, and done, and well done
And thus I end what was begun.
To the Three Holy Kindreds I give thanks
To the Lord of Wisdom I give thanks
To the Mother of All I give thanks
Thus do I remember the work of the wise.

Exercise 1: The Road to the Inner Grove

This work develops a personal habit and inner ritual of vision journey that allows you to easily reach your Inner working space – the Inner Grove in which you will do several works. This script is offered as an example, though it can be used as written.

• *Seat yourself comfortably upright, back straight.*

• *Work a short blessing of the space, or the full Grove opening and Gate if you wish - in your first exercises it might be best to work the full opening, with the Gate.*

• *Renew and strengthen your Earth and Heavens contacts.*

• *Feel the cool Earth Power and the hot Sky Power meet in your head, meet in your heart, and meet in your loins.*

• *And from the meeting-places, feel the mingling of the Powers flow out into your whole form — into your hands, into your form, into your eyes. Where you have eyes of flesh, so you now have eyes of vision.*

• *Open your eyes of vision, and use your memory of the setting of your Shrine and tools. As you remember them, envision them, so that it is as if you see them with open eyes. It is the eyes of vision that open in this way, and it is in the eyes of vision that you will move.*

• *With your material eyes closed, decide to stand in your vision form. Allow your eyes to rise, effortlessly. You rise to your natural height, and take a moment to gaze upon your Shrine and Hallows as if you had stood in flesh. Allow the details of your Shrine to become clear.*

- *And in the meeting-places, feel the mingling of the Powers begin to produce the Mist - the streams of vapor pouring out of your Inner Cauldrons, flowing out from the roots of the Tree, where Fire and Water meet.*

- *visualize the Mist gathering and thickening, beginning to accumulate. The Mist gathers, growing thicker, and collecting around your feet... around your hips and loins... around your arms and chest. It grows thick and opaque, and rises, at last, to surround your head.*

- *Now, standing in the Mist, it is time to begin... in your imagination's eye... in your Inner Vision... not with your physical body... but with the* will of your mind and your power of vision... you create the Gate Sign before you.You remember the presence of the Threshold landscape that you have visited before...

- With your awareness firmly centered in your vision-self, step forward toward the Sign... and step through the Sign..., and steo out of the Mist... the Mist thins away... now, with memory and will... you see the scene resolve before you... your goal-image, your Nemeton, revealed in its Otherworld form... elements of the place you left behind in the common world... it resolve in your Inner Eye...You behold the Inner Grove resolving before you... you see the details more clearly now...

The Return

- Standing in vision in your Grove... remember your body... where it sits before the Hallows in the common world... Look out to the edge of your Grove, and there, see the Gate Sign appear... and the Mist beyond it... walk across the Grove, and passeasily through the Sign, remembering your body as your goal... and step out before your Fire in your common Hallows...

- Remember your Hallows, and see yourself seated there before them... go to your body... turn, and step backward into the space where your body is sitting... raise your spirit-hand before you... and make a tuathal triskel in the air before you... sit down into your body... renew your center... feel the Earth and Sky Powers meeting in your flesh...

-Remember your body, and let your awareness be firmly behind your eyes... feel the air flow in your lungs... the blood course in your veins... remember all you have seen and done in this work... open your eyes, and know that your spirit has returned fully to your flesh... stretch... and be finished with the trance.

Exercise 2: Building the Inner Grove

- Come to your Shrine or Hallows, Bless all and open a gate.
- Use your Short Road to the Grove:

> **Rise in Vision, and see your Hallows**
> **Call the Mist**
> **Make the Gate Sign**
> **Step through the Gate Sign into the Grove**
> **Envision and remember the Grove**

- So you come again into the Grove... you pass through the gate and onto the ground of your Threshold locale... and allow the scene to resolve before you... remember where you have placed your Well... your Hearth of the Sacred Fire... see the World-tree as it stands in this small personal place...

- you have been working with forms for your Inner Hallows... now you must choose how you will build and shape them, for your next phase of work... a Well... a pillar or Tree... the Fire in the Tintean... Simple or grand, earth-mound or golden temple... you will decide and create... as you begin to envision the shaping and detail of your Inner Grove...

- You might begin with the Well... for no place is whole without fresh water... go to the Well you have seen before... and consider what a more ideal form might be... what shape would inspire you?... go then to the Fire, as it has been before... envision what a true altar for your own Inner Fire might be... and turn to see the Tree or Bile as it has appeared... and consider how you would see its presence here before you...

- Let them be built by your will and vision... consider the bricks and stones, the substance and color... note how the things you build combine with the images of nature or environment present in the space... images of your own hands placing the materials may enter your mind... but it is by will and vision and shaping that you determine the form that your Grove will keep for some time to come... spend some while at this work...

...

- Now, in your vision body, turn and look around you... turn to your right... and to your left... turn at last and look behind you... you note clearly the form and nature of the things you are building... see them

again, your Inner Sacred Grove... as you look at the Inner World around
you...

The Return

- *Standing in vision in your Grove... remember your body... where it sits before the Hallows in the common world... Look out to the edge of your Grove, and there, see the Gate Sign appear... and the Mist beyond it... walk across the Grove, and pass easily through the Sign, remembering your body as your goal... and step out before your Fire in your common Hallows...*

- *Remember your Hallows, and see yourself seated there before them... go to your body... turn, and step backward into the space where your body is sitting... raise your spirit-hand before you... and make a tuathal triskel in the air before you... sit down into your body... renew your center... feel the Earth and Sky Powers meeting in your flesh...*

- *Remember your body, and let your awareness be firmly behind your eyes... feel the air flow in your lungs... the blood course in your veins... remember all you have seen and done in this work... open your eyes, and know that your spirit has returned fully to your flesh... stretch... and be finished with the trance.*

Exercise 3: Working in the Inner Grove

- Come to your Shrine or Hallows, Bless all and open a gate.
- Use your Short Road to the Grove:

> **Rise in Vision, and see your Hallows**
> **Call the Mist**
> **Make the Gate Sign**
> **Step through the Gate Sign into the Grove**
> **Envision and remember the Grove**

- Remember and re-establish the Inner Hallows, and the surrounding environment.

- Stand at your Inner Fire, and bring the Two Powers into your vision body... hold up your hands, and know that whatever sacrifice you have given in the common world will also be available to you here in the Threshold... so make your usual offerings to the Hallows, and speak as you will...

- Let silver come to your hand... and give it, a substance of yourself, to the Well... and speak in the voice of your vision...

- Let precious scented oil come to your hand... and give it, a substance of yourself, to the Fire... and speak in the voice of your vision...

- Let burning herbs and pure water come into your two hands... and with them, substance of yourself, honor the Tree, sprinkling its roots and perfuming its leaves... and speak in the voice of your vision...

- pause and feel the presence of the place... its weight and solidity... its weirdness and limnality... remember...

- It is proper to do any other small bits of ritual you wish here before the Inner Fire...

The Return

- Standing in vision in your Grove... remember your body... where it sits before the Hallows in the common world... Look out to the edge of your Grove, and there, see the Gate Sign appear... and the Mist beyond it... walk across the Grove, and passeasily through the Sign, remembering your body as your goal... and step out before your Fire in your common Hallows...

- *Remember your Hallows, and see yourself seated there before them... go to your body... turn, and step backward into the space where your body is sitting... raise your spirit-hand before you... and make a tuathal triskel in the air before you... sit down into your body... renew your center... feel the Earth and Sky Powers meeting in your flesh...*

-*Remember your body, and let your awareness be firmly behind your eyes... feel the air flow in your lungs... the blood course in your veins... remember all you have seen and done in this work... open your eyes, and know that your spirit has returned fully to your flesh... stretch... and be finished with the trance.*

The

Fifth Cycle

Working In Vision

The Fifth Cycle - The Endless Road

In magic the arts of meditation and vision most clearly bridge the gap between practical magic and the work of spiritual awareness. In many kinds of mysticism the primary goal of mental practice is to train and focus the mind in order to achieve the divine awarenesses central to the specific system. On the other hand we find spell-craft that is worked entirely with mental effort, especially the many kinds of energetic healing practice.

The practices of the first four cycles of this work will provide a solid basic skill for any of these goals. Those who choose to actively practice these arts will have many choices available to them. As with everything in magic, personal preference will determine whether the Druid tends toward ritual or meditation, vision or silence. Wisdom recommends balance, and if one's tendency is to action and deed it is good to practice silence, and vice-versa.

This final cycle offers paths both practical and mystical. The work of traveling in vision Provides an entire method of dealing with the spirits, separate from but compatible with ritual spirit-arte. Through the meeting of spirits in the Three Worlds, using the basic launch patterns provided, many kinds of practical magic can be worked. The work of vision allows us to approach the Gods more directly as well. All considerations of practical effects in the world aside, to draw near to the Gods in vision is to be warmed by their Fire, immersed in their Flow. The common self does not emerge from such events unaffected. In the final section of this cycle we address a powerful spiritual symbol that brings us directly into the realm of the mystical. We map an approach to that aspect of the divine that dwells in each of us individually. This has been called many names over the centuries, including Agathodaimon, but here I have concocted an Irish name for this esoteric concept.

On another level, the whole work of vision-journeying and Threshold awareness has an important general mystical content. Our common lives are an entanglement of mind and matter, habit and impulse, social coercion and personal programming. To take up the work of magic is, at least to some degree, to take in hand the vehicle in which we ride. In the Threshold we are, for a while, in a realm in which our will can work directly, a world that we more consciously make. To gain this power is itself to touch the Divine In You. Can it be a leap too far to discover that not only the Threshold, but the entire cosmos is in fact a construction of the mind?

Exploring the Otherworld –
Self-Generating Trance Journeys

With the completion of the Inner Grove Threshold locale we can begin independent or self-generated Inner Journeys. We will provide a few more guided trances, including techniques for vision and inspiration, and in this month we will provide a core pattern that can serve as a ramp-up to independent vision of any kind. In this way we are moving from the realm of "guided meditation" into that of "shamanic journeying" to use popular terms.

The process of self-guiding is driven by alternating active imagination with a deliberate openness to new input. You will begin as we have been working, moving from one memorized symbol to another. In the next phase you will set forth into the mist, beyond the trees you can see, into landscapes that must resolve themselves around you even as landscapes do in a walk through the forest or city.

The Mist-vision is one basic method of approaching the need for self-resolving environments. You can proceed through the Mist, until some symbol or glimpse of a locale appears. Do not demand too much of yourself in terms of 'objectivity' or externality in these first stages. When your inner vision shows you an opening, allow your active imagination to grab hold. In many ways this kind of vision begins by trusting your imagination to give you true vision of Threshold reality and beyond. In the Inner our imagination is as much to be trusted as our eyes in the material world.

So, you might help yourself resolve locale out of the misty potential by asking yourself "If I could see through the Mist, what would the place look like?" or "If I were nearing my goal, where would I be?" Allow yourself to simply envision what it would be, and so, let it be. As you move forward, encounter beings, and see new things you are seeking that moment when the vision is proceeding with you, but not being driven by you. It is such moments that are the gate of the Otherworld beyond the Threshold.

Symbol-transition is another traditional way to enter an unplanned locale. You simply envision the Gate-sign, and within it whatever symbol you hope will take you to your desired place. By rising in your Inner Vision and passing through the symbol, the locale simply resolves around you. This can be done with known symbols, such as Runes or Ogham letters (or tree-leaves), but it can also be done with unknown signs, perhaps the symbols on the curbstone of Brugh na Boyne, or the panels of the Gundestrup Cauldron. In this way you can explore the Otherworld, always able to return to your

Inner Grove safe space.

In this work you will perform a few basic explorations, seeking to gain skill in unguided journeying. You will find doors that can lead deep beneath the surface of your Threshold land, and high above it, as well as simply setting forth into the land surrounding it. If you are working a complete system of Pagan magic, such as the Nine Moons, or this work combined with the work of the Book of Summoning, you will have the aid of your allies, who can be perhaps the best guides. With a Teacher among the Dead and the Familiar among the Landwights you will have much more experienced and powerful support

.

Roads From the Inner Grove
1: The Door of the Deep
- *Come to your Shrine or Hallows, Bless all and open a gate.*
- *Perform the Nineteen Working, paying good attention to the Da Fein invocation.*
- *Use your Short Road to the Grove:*

Between Fire and Water, I find my balance
From the Union of Fire and Water the Mist rises
Let the Mist carry me, and my Eye of Vision open
Let the Eye lead me, and my vision be clear and true
Let my Vision enchant me, with the sorcerer's sight
Eye of Vision, eye of flesh, let me see clearly
That the Work of the Wise be done.

- *Remember and re-establish the Inner Hallows, and the surrounding environment.*
- *Stand at your Inner Fire, and bring the Two Powers into your vision body... hold up your hands, and know that whatever sacrifice you have given in the common world will also be available to you here in the Threshold... so make your usual offerings to the Hallows, and speak as you will...*
- *Let silver come to your hand... and give it, a substance of yourself, to the Well... and speak in the voice of your vision...*
- *Let precious scented oil come to your hand... and give it, a substance of yourself, to the Fire... and speak in the voice of your vision...*
- *Let burning herbs and pure water come into your two hands... and with them, substance of yourself, honor the Tree, sprinkling its roots and perfuming its leaves... and speak in the voice of your vision...*
- *pause and feel the presence of the place... its weight and solidity... its weirdness and limnality... remember...*
- *Now turn your attention outward, to the edges of your formal space... see the natural environment in which your Grove rests... step away from the Hallows, and walk toward the edge, looking around, noting detail...*
- *As you turn again, you notice an opening in the rock or soil... a cave, or a carved portal, or simply a hole in the earth... you draw near, curious,*

and you understand that this is a door for you... an entry to the greater world beneath...

-You decide to enter, and discover that it is easy to step into the opening... a few steps in and the light of your Grove is left behind... and you find yourself walking down a spiral... turning rightward... walking downward... through darkness... until you arrive at a dimly lit chamber, deep beneath the land...

- The small room is undecorated, but you see that it could be a chapel or retreat, down at the edge of the deep... in one wall is a door... and on the door a sign... you may be able to see it clearly, or may be you cannot... but a strange light shines around the crack of the door in the dimness of your antechamber...

- You walk to the door, and once again see the sign upon it... your stretch out your hand, and open the door... and behold the Underworld beyond... you pause and observe as the scene comes into better focus... and you step through the open door...

- A small porch of stone is beneath your feet... and around you is a landscape of the Otherworld... of the Underworld Lands... let it resolve into greater clarity... see it, hear it...

- If you wish, you may step away from the door... walk a little, entering the world you have seen... you may see beings... may even speak with one... but for now be calm and polite, and make no promises, nor accept any... as you explore, a bit, this locale...

- ...

- But for now, you must return to the common world... and so you turn, and remember the locale from which you came, and the small room with the door in it... remember the sign upon it... you move, walking, and around a bend is the door with the small stone portico...

-You open the door, if it has closed, and you step through it... into the small, dark antechamber... and begin to climb the steps... upward, turning leftward... rising from the dark toward the light... and arriving at last at the opening to your Inner Grove...

-You step out, into the weird light of the Threshold... before you in the center are the Hallows of your Inner Grove... And, standing in vision in your Grove... remember your body... where it sits before the Hallows in the common world... Look out to the edge of your Grove, and there, see the Gate Sign appear... and the Mist beyond it... walk across the Grove, and pass easily through the Sign, remembering your body as your goal... and step out before your Fire in your common Hallows...

- Remember your Hallows, and see yourself seated there before them... go to your body... turn, and step backward into the space where your body is sitting... raise your spirit-hand before you... and make a tuathal triskel in the air before you... sit down into your body... renew your center... feel the Earth and Sky Powers meeting in your flesh...

-Remember your body, and let your awareness be firmly behind your eyes... feel the air flow in your lungs... the blood course in your veins... remember all you have seen and done in this work... open your eyes, and know that your spirit has returned fully to your flesh... stretch... and be finished with the trance.

2: The Door of the Sky

- Come to your Shrine or Hallows, Bless all and open a gate.
- Perform the Nineteen Working, paying good attention to the Da Fein invocation.
- Use your Short Road to the Grove:

Between Fire and Water, I find my balance
From the Union of Fire and Water the Mist rises
Let the Mist carry me, and my Eye of Vision open
Let the Eye lead me, and my vision be clear and true
Let my Vision enchant me, with the sorcerer's sight
Eye of Vision, eye of flesh, let me see clearly
That the Work of the Wise be done.

- Remember and re-establish the Inner Hallows, and the surrounding environment.
- Stand at your Inner Fire, and bring the Two Powers into your vision body... hold up your hands, and know that whatever sacrifice you have given in the common world will also be available to you here in the Threshold... so make your usual offerings to the Hallows, and speak as

129

you will...

- Let silver come to your hand... and give it, a substance of yourself, to theWell... and speak in the voice of your vision...

- Let precious scented oil come to your hand... and give it, a substance of yourself, to the Fire... and speak in the voice of your vision...

- Let burning herbs and pure water come into your two hands... and with them, substance of yourself, honor the Tree, sprinkling its roots and perfuming its leaves... and speak in the voice of your vision...

- pause and feel the presence of the place... its weight and solidity... its weirdness and limnality... remember...

- Now turn your attention to the center of your Sacred Grove... there stands the Pillar of the Grove, the World Tree in your Threshold holy place... step toward the Hallows, and walk around the Bile, seeing its form, noting detail...

- As you turn again, you notice that upon the surface of the Pillar... the Tree... is cut a set of stairs... narrow and steep, at first, leading upward along the pillar... You find that you can set a foot upon the bottom step... and then another... and you are climbing, up the spiraling stair around the World Tree...

- Turning rightward... you climb upward... the smoke of the fire swirling around you... smoke becoming cloud... as you rise above the Grove... until you arrive at a misty chamber, high above the land...

- The small room is undecorated, for now, but you see that it could be a chapel or retreat, high at the top of the Pillar... in one wall is a door... and on the door a sign... you may be able to see it clearly, or may be you cannot... but you see a strange shining around the crack of the door in the misty brightness of your antechamber...

- You walk to the door, and once again see the sign upon it... your stretch out your hand, and open the door... and behold the Heavens beyond... you pause and observe as the scene comes into better focus... and you step through the open door...

- A small porch of stone is beneath your feet... and around you is a landscape of the Otherworld... of the Heavenly Lands... let it resolve

into greater clarity... see it, hear it...

- If you wish, you may step away from the door... walk a little, entering the world you have seen... you may see beings... may even speak with one... but for now be calm and polite, and make no promises, nor accept any... as you explore, a bit, this locale...

- ...

- But for now, you must return to the common world... and so you turn, and remember the locale from which you came, and the small room with the door in it... remember the sign upon it... you move, walking, and around a bend is the door with the small stone portico...

- You open the door, if it has closed, and you step through it... into the misty antechamber... and begin to climb down the steps... downward, turning leftward... down the windy trunk of the Great Pillar... and arriving at last at the base of the Bile, in your Inner Grove...

- You step out, into the weird light of the Threshold Fire... step out and stand before the Hallows of your Inner Grove... And, standing in vision in your Grove... remember your body... where it sits before the Hallows in the common world... Look out to the edge of your Grove, and there, see the Gate Sign appear... and the Mist beyond it... walk across the Grove, and pass easily through the Sign, remembering your body as your goal... and step out before your Fire in your common Hallows...

- Remember your Hallows, and see yourself seated there before them... go to your body... turn, and step backward into the space where your body is sitting... raise your spirit-hand before you... and make a tuathal triskel in the air before you... sit down into your body... renew your center... feel the Earth and Sky Powers meeting in your flesh...

- Remember your body, and let your awareness be firmly behind your eyes... feel the air flow in your lungs... the blood course in your veins... remember all you have seen and done in this work... open your eyes, and know that your spirit has returned fully to your flesh... stretch... and be finished with the trance

3: The Middle Door

- *Come to your Shrine or Hallows, Bless all and open a gate.*
- *Perform the Nineteen Working, paying good attention to the Da Fein invocation.*
- *Use your Short Road to the Grove:*

Between Fire and Water, I find my balance
From the Union of Fire and Water the Mist rises
Let the Mist carry me, and my Eye of Vision open
Let the Eye lead me, and my vision be clear and true
Let my Vision enchant me, with the sorcerer's sight
Eye of Vision, eye of flesh, let me see clearly
That the Work of the Wise be done.

- *Remember and re-establish the Inner Hallows, and the surrounding environment.*
- *Stand at your Inner Fire, and bring the Two Powers into your vision body... hold up your hands, and know that whatever sacrifice you have given in the common world will also be available to you here in the Threshold... so make your usual offerings to the Hallows, and speak as you will...*

Let silver come to your hand... and give it, a substance of yourself, to the Well... and speak in the voice of your vision...

- *Let burning herbs and pure water come into your two hands... and with them, substance of yourself, honor the Tree, sprinkling its roots and perfuming its leaves... and speak in the voice of your vision...*

pause and feel the presence of the place... its weight and solidity... its weirdness and limnality... remember...

You stand in your Inner Grove, from which you have already traveled to the Threshold of both the Underworld and the Heavens... yet your Grove already stands in a realm of many wonders... you have built your Grove on the Threshold of the Middle World...

Stand and turn once around, and see the setting in which your Grove is built... Walk to the edge, and begin to circle the area... turning your right shoulder to your Fire... see the trees or stones or plain... and walk again around the Hallows... observing... passing each feature again...

Turn again, rightward, around your Grove, and a gate or door will make itself clear to you... this is one Gate to the Middle Realm... the realm of wonder and story... where so many of the Spirits dwell, and where the Gods meet mortal dreams...

The door may be a physical door, or a tangle in the green, or a slit in the rock, but it will call to you... and it will bear, somewhere on it... a sign... that makes it plain that it is the road that you should take...

you step through the door, and make your way through a short, dark place... and emerge onto a small clearing... in the Middle Realm.

If you wish, you may step away from the door... walk a little, entering the world you have seen... you may see beings... may even speak with one... but for now be calm and polite, and make no promises, nor accept any... as you explore, a bit, this locale...

...

But for now, you must return to the common world... and so you turn, and remember the locale from which you came, and the narrow, dark passage... remember the sign upon it... you move, walking, and around a bend is the door with the small clearing...

- You open the door, if it has closed, and you step through it... into the short, dark passage... and emerge into your Grove... once again, circle your Hallows, right shoulder to the Fire... and then return to the Sacred Center... arriving at last at the Fire, Well and Tree, in your Inner Grove...

- You stand in the the warm light of the Threshold Fire... and, standing in vision in your Grove... remember your body... where it sits before your Hallows in the common world... Look out to the edge of your Grove, and there, see the Gate Sign of the common world appear... and the Mist beyond it... walk across the Grove, and pass easily through the Sign, remembering your body as your goal... and step out before your Fire in your common Hallows...

- Remember your Hallows, and see yourself seated there before them... go to your body... turn, and step backward into the space where your body is sitting... raise your spirit-hand before you... and make a tuathal triskel in the air before you... sit down into your body... renew your center... feel

133

the Earth and Sky Powers meeting in your flesh...

-Remember your body, and let your awareness be firmly behind your eyes...
feel the air flow in your lungs... the blood course in your veins... remember
all you have seen and done in this work... open your eyes, and know that
your spirit has returned fully to your flesh... stretch... and be finished
with the trance

• The Shrine of the Da Fein
The Vision of the Divine In Me

In this final series of trances we use the skill of Vision to seek the Da Fein – the image or presence of the spark of the divine in you. If you have been practicing the Nineteen Working in full you have been opening yourself to the Da Fein, acknowledging it and uniting with it in contemplation. Perhaps you have some experiences of the presence of that being, that power. By using the Threshold vision you can sharpen and objectify your experience of the divine in you, making a more direct knowledge and conversation possible.

The wise have long debated the question of whether the God of Myself exists as a separate being from the spirit of a mortal as a companion and guide, or whether it is the truest 'Self' of mortal existence, intrinsic to the soul. No definitive answer has been reached, nor is it likely to be. For the sake of this work we will approach the Da Fein as a separate thing or person, a goal of our spiritual journey. In this we follow the method taught by tradition, from the magical storytellers of the north to Classical theurgic ritual. It is by making an image of a spiritual power, formed in the proper way, and calling the presence of that power to dwell in that image that we do the work of both magic and religion. In many cases this work is grounded in a material idol or symbol of the spirit. The Da Fein has no better eidolon than the living body of the Druid. It is through meditation, such as the Nineteen Work, that the Da Fein is embodied in the self. It is through vision that its form and voice become clear.

These trance scripts use a detailed opening description to deepen trance and lead firmly into Threshold awareness. The simple images of transition – the forest, the door, the shrine – open out into the actual work of experiencing the presence of the Da Fein. Allow me to advise you to approach this with a minimum of expectations and an open mind to whatever symbols and images may present themselves. Even though we discuss some traditional forms and concepts of the Divine In the Self, be prepared to be surprised, and be prepared to accept what comes. It is in those visions that the moens and glimpses of the Divine past the Threshold are to be discovered.

For a student working doing the work of Druidry as a spiritual path these exercises can open crucial ways and understandings. I think that they will also serve any Pagan who hopes to deepen the connection with the divine and empower personal magic.

Three Forms of the Da Fein

It is worthwhile to spend some time simply being open to the feel and presence of the Da Fein, listening for its voice and counsel. In this book we present the Nineteen Working as a balanced meditative work of wisdom and power, that culminates with the contemplation of the Divine within the self. This is the mystical core of the Da Fein, but there is practical magic application as well. One of the powers of the Da Fein is as an actual voice of counsel, a source of guidance in the work of magic. Tradition gives no firm notion of how the Pagan Celts might have visualized or symbolized such a spiritual power as the God of Myself. I offer several possible models drawn from Celtic symbolism. Consider working your way through these and whatever other notions may occur as you experiment with the exercise.

1: The Graal: Both ancient Gaelic story and later, Celtic-influenced romances present the image of a magical vessel which confers a variety of blessings upon those who come into its presence or drink from it. The Book of Invasions tells of the Dagda's Cauldron of Wonder, which gave every feaster his favorite food. Dian Cecht, the physician of the Tuatha De, kept a Cauldron (or Well) of Healing that raised dead warriors to fight again. British tales remember the famous Cauldron of Inspiration, which made the poet Taliesin, and the Red Woman's Cauldron, which, again, raised the Dead. So, we find a triple-cauldron complex – Healing, Sustenance and Inspiration - rather different from our poetic Cauldrons. This is the Secret Presence itself, the Poet's Gift, the Mead of Inspiration, the Vessel of Three Drops. Whether bronze-age cauldron, iron-age drinking horn or medieval chalice, you may find a vision of the Vessel of Blessings, and perhaps of the Shrine or Chapel in which it sits to be productive.

2: The Shining Presence: It is common in all cultures to see this sort of being – this Personal Theos – in anthropomorphic form. Several cultural systems present us with personal guardian spirits, so attached to us as to be a part of us, yet still separate entities from anything we could call 'ourselves'. We can approach such a spirit by making an image in which it can reside, in a temple in our hearts. In some cultures it is plainly said that the Personal God is of the opposite gender to the mortal self, in others this isn't plainly so. There may be some value in that sort of vision of a beautiful messenger, even in tying the power of eros to our efforts to draw near to the divine. Others may find the figure of an Elder or of a Child, of either gender, useful. In all this is it good to begin with some experimental figure, but then to be open to what the mind and heart may reveal.

3: The Speaking Flame, the Speaking Well: As you build your Druidic practice you will develop an Inner Grove, a personal sacred space from which you might set off into other visions. In this you will make your Fire Altar and Well of the Deep, at your own Boundary Tree. Beneath and within the landscape of your Inner Grove you might conceive a deeper shrine, a secret place known only to you, in which you find a stranger Fire and Well, that may act as the eye and voice of a powerful spirit being. You can explore this setting and work with it in a variety of ways, from approaching the Voices as oracles, asking questions and hearing answers, or as ways to make Inner offerings, especially to the Da Fein itself.

Of course these images may be mixed and matched as you find inspirational. The goal is to find a symbol that conveys the presence of the Divine in a way outside the common list of Gods and Spirits, in ways meaningful and powerful to the Druid. We make the images, and open our hearts, and the Da Fein flows and shines in the images we provide. In those images we then seek to hear the voice of the Da Fein, and be heard by it. In time we seek to be intimate with this most personal of Allies in every spiritual way, open to the Wisdom of the Divine In Us.

In truth you can spend as much time as you like exploring this state, which can produce a powerful expansion of awareness. When your work leads you to begin approaching the Da Fein you may wish to work this exercise separately from the longer Cosmos vision and contemplation. However there is power in the finding of the secret place of the Da Fein deep within the Cosmos you have worked, as presented in the complete Nineteen Working. In establishing the center of your Divine Self amidst the Cosmos, you open yourself to the deepest connection with the Dance of Being. You may not achieve 'results' immediately – like any work, it is ongoing work itself that brings the result. To hold the whole Great Pattern of the Nineteen Working meditation – the Silence, the Two, the Three and the Four, the Nine and the One Other is a powerful work of mystical vision.

The Secret Shrine

1: The Door of the Shrine

- Come to your Shrine or Hallows, Bless all and open a gate.
- Perform the Nineteen Working, paying good attention to the Da Fein invocation.
- Use your Short Road to the Grove:

Between Fire and Water, I find my balance
From the Union of Fire and Water the Mist rises
Let the Mist carry me, and my Eye of Vision open
Let the Eye lead me, and my vision be clear and true
Let my Vision enchant me, with the sorcerer's sight
Eye of Vision, eye of flesh, let me see clearly
That the Work of the Wise be done.

- *Stand at your Inner Fire, and bring the Two Powers into your vision body... hold up your hands, and know that whatever sacrifice you have given in the common world will also be available to you here in the Threshold... so make your usual offerings to the Hallows, and speak as you will...*
- *Let silver come to your hand... and give it, a substance of yourself, to the Well... and speak in the voice of your vision...*
- *Let precious scented oil come to your hand... and give it, a substance of yourself, to the Fire... and speak in the voice of your vision...*
- *Let burning herbs and pure water come into your two hands... and with them, substance of yourself, honor the Tree, sprinkling its roots and perfuming its leaves... and speak in the voice of your vision...*
- *pause and feel the presence of the place... its weight and solidity... its weirdness and limnality... remember...*
- *Somewhere deep within the Threshold is the vision of your own secret shrine, a place where you can meet your Da Fein face to face, as you would an ally. Stand before your Inner Hallows, and gaze across the Fire toward your Gate. Make an invocation of your Da Fein, as your understanding guides you, calling to the God In You to send you a symbol, a sigil, a sign*

by which you might journey to its own secret shrine.

- Let the sign resolve before you, becoming clear in the gate... let it be as if the Gate were before you, as if it were one with the Inner Hallows... step forward, and pass through the Gate...

- Now a path or a passage will appear to you... and you will follow it... for as long as you need... deeper into the Inner realms... remember as you go, what sights you see... for it is this path that will lead you again, to the Secret Shrine...

- At last you arrive at a further gate... a Gate well-closed with solid doors... see the doors before you... see what substance they are made of... see what signs they may bear...

- Even the presence of these Doors seems a wonder to you, and you are filled with joy at your discovery... but for now you will come no further... raise your hands and greet the Da Fein from outside the shrine, for you will return here again, and if all is well, the Doors will be open to you...

- And remember... remember again the road from your Grove to these Doors, for you must try to return the same way, tomorrow...

The Return

- Now, as you prepare to finish your work, remember... remember all that you have seen and done... all that you have learned...

- Turn and return the way your came, marking the landmarks of your journey... see the Gate before you with the sign of your Grove upon it, and pass through to emerge in your own Inner Grove...

- And, standing in vision in your Grove... remember your body... where it sits before the Hallows in the common world... Look out to the edge of your Grove, and there, see the Gate Sign appear... and the Mist beyond it... walk across the Grove, and passeasily through the Sign, remembering your body as your goal... and step out before your Fire in your common Hallows...

- Remember your Hallows, and see yourself seated there before them... go to your body... turn, and step backward into the space where your body is sitting... raise your spirit-hand before you... and make a tuathal triskel in the air before you... sit down into your body... renew your center... feel the Earth and Sky Powers meeting in your flesh...

-Remember your body, and let your awareness be firmly behind your eyes... feel the air flow in your lungs... the blood course in your veins... remember all you have seen and done in this work... open your eyes, and know that your spirit has returned fully to your flesh... stretch... and be finished with the trance.

2: Seeking the Secret Shrine

- Come to your Shrine or Hallows, Bless all and open a gate.
- Perform the Nineteen Working, paying good attention to the Da Fein invocation.
- Use your Short Road to the Grove:

Between Fire and Water, I find my balance
From the Union of Fire and Water the Mist rises
Let the Mist carry me, and my Eye of Vision open
Let the Eye lead me, and my vision be clear and true
Let my Vision enchant me, with the sorcerer's sight
Eye of Vision, eye of flesh, let me see clearly
That the Work of the Wise be done.

- Stand at your Inner Fire, and bring the Two Powers into your vision body... hold up your hands, and know that whatever sacrifice you have given in the common world will also be available to you here in the Threshold... so make your usual offerings to the Hallows, and speak as you will...

... ...

- pause and feel the presence of the place... its weight and solidity... its weirdness and limnality... remember...
- Now you seek again your own secret shrine, by the road you have learned. Stand before your Inner Hallows, and gaze across the Fire toward your Gate. Make an invocation of your Da Fein, as your understanding guides you, calling to the God In You. - Let the sign resolve before you, becoming clear in the gate... let it be as if the Gate were before you, as if it were one with the Inner Hallows... step forward, and pass through the Gate...

- Again the path appears to you... and you follow it... remember the way, and see again the landmarks and images of the way to the Shrine...
... ...

- At last you arrive at a further gate... a Gate well-closed with solid doors... see the doors before you... see what substance they are made of... see what signs they may bear...

- Even the presence of these Doors seems a wonder to you, and you raise your hands and greet the Da Fein from outside the shrine... and the Doors of the Secret Shrine open to you...

- So you may go into the Shrine... to call to the Da Fein... to speak to it and listen for its answer...

- So... allow the Secret Shrine to appear around you... and behold before you the form of Your God, the Da Fein... light and shadow... nature and wonder... see the face... the eyes, the mouth... the symbols the figure may bear... the details of the Shrine in which the throne and altar is set...

- Perhaps there is a presence within, perhaps only symbols and signs... so remember... remember the form and color, the symbol and shape of this Shrine...

- You have come to find the seat and altar of your own Inner God — the spirit of you that keeps your way and work, even when your common mind knows it not... the spirit some that some call the servant, some call the master and some call holy luck...

- For a time abide in this vision... call out to the Da Fein as your inspiration Guides you... and remember... remember...

The Return

- Now, as you prepare to finish your work, remember... remember all that you have seen and done... all that you have learned...

- Bid farewell to you Da Fein, whether or not you have seen it plainly... affirm your desire to know and understand the Divine In You...

- Turn away, and again follow the path back toward your Grove... summon the Gate and the sign of your own Inner Grove... gathering your will, step forward through that Gate, and return to your Grove...

- *And, standing in vision in your Grove... remember your body... where it sits before the Hallows in the common world... Look out to the edge of your Grove, and there, see the Gate Sign appear... and the Mist beyond it... walk across the Grove, and pass easily through the Sign, remembering your body as your goal... and step out before your Fire in your common Hallows...*

- *Remember your Hallows, and see yourself seated there before them... go to your body... turn, and step backward into the space where your body is sitting... raise your spirit-hand before you... and make a tuathal triskel in the air before you... sit down into your body... renew your center... feel the Earth and Sky Powers meeting in your flesh...*

- *Remember your body, and let your awareness be firmly behind your eyes... feel the air flow in your lungs... the blood course in your veins... remember all you have seen and done in this work... open your eyes, and know that your spirit has returned fully to your flesh... stretch... and be finished with the trance.*

3: The Face of the Da Fein

- *Come to your Shrine or Hallows, Bless all and open a gate.*
- *Perform the Nineteen Working, paying good attention to the Da Fein invocation.*
- *Use your Short Road to the Grove:*

Between Fire and Water, I find my balance
From the Union of Fire and Water the Mist rises
Let the Mist carry me, and my Eye of Vision open
Let the Eye lead me, and my vision be clear and true
Let my Vision enchant me, with the sorcerer's sight
Eye of Vision, eye of flesh, let me see clearly
That the Work of the Wise be done.

- *Stand at your Inner Fire, and bring the Two Powers into your vision body... hold up your hands, and know that whatever sacrifice you have given in the common world will also be available to you here in the Threshold... so make your usual offerings to the Hallows, and speak as you will...*

... ...

- pause and feel the presence of the place... its weight and solidity... its weirdness and limnality... remember...

- Now call to your Allies... take a moment to know their presence at your sides, in whatever way they manifest to you... throughout, you may speak with them, and perhaps they will guide you, or perhaps simply join you in your journey...

- Now gaze across the Hallows to the Gate, and see again the sign of your Secret Shrine... where you can meet your Da Fein face to face, as you would an ally. Stand before your Inner Hallows, and gaze across the Fire toward your Gate. Open your heart to your Da Fein, as your understanding guides you, calling to the God In You as you step forward, and pass through the Gate, opening your heart and spirit to the God In You...

- To go to the Shrine... along the path...

- To arrive at the Doors, and pass within... to call to the Da Fein... to speak to it and listen for its answer...

- So... allow the Secret Shrine to appear around you... and behold before you the form of Your God, the Da Fein... light and shadow... nature and wonder... see the face... the eyes, the mouth... the symbols the figure may bear... the details of the Shrine in which the throne and altar is set...

- And in this time you can ask your Good Spirit for its name, and it's sign, and its powers and station, just as you have your allies... and the Da Fein may answer...

- From there any conversation may be possible... ask and listen, speak and hear, as you stand in the presence of the God of Your Spirit...
The Return

- Now, as you prepare to finish your work, remember... remember all that you have seen and done... all that you have learned...

- Bid farewell to your Da Fein, whether or not you have seen it plainly... affirm your desire to know and understand the Divine In You...

143

- Turn away, and summon the Gate and the sign of your own Inner Grove... gathering your will, step forward through that Gate, and return to your Grove...

- And, standing in vision in your Grove... remember your body... where it sits before the Hallows in the common world... Look out to the edge of your Grove, and there, see the Gate Sign appear... and the Mist beyond it... walk across the Grove, and pass easily through the Sign, remembering your body as your goal... and step out before your Fire in your common Hallows...

- Remember your Hallows, and see yourself seated there before them... go to your body... turn, and step backward into the space where your body is sitting... raise your spirit-hand before you... and make a tuathal triskel in the air before you... sit down into your body... renew your center... feel the Earth and Sky Powers meeting in your flesh...

- Remember your body, and let your awareness be firmly behind your eyes... feel the air flow in your lungs... the blood course in your veins... remember all you have seen and done in this work... open your eyes, and know that your spirit has returned fully to your flesh... stretch... and be finished with the trance.

The Gate of Vision

Celtic lore teaches that those things that are neither one thing nor another, neither one place or time nor the other have a special potential for access to the Otherworld and the application of magic. So rites are worked at twilight, neither day nor night, at the shores of the Sea or the tops of hills, where Land and Sky meet. Sacred places were kept on the boundaries between tribal lands, claimed by none but the spirits. As always, magic art is the application of such natural laws deliberately, for willed goals. So when we wish to create a place of between-ness we can simply define ourselves as 'here', and create a door that leads to 'there'. By standing in that door we partake of its neither-nor power, and by passing through we use that power to enter the Threshold.

One of the most direct traditional methods for launching the awareness past guided imagery into the Threshold is the vision of the Gate. In all cultures, wherever humankind has built a house, or set aside a clearing in the forest, or built a wall of protection, the gate becomes the natural symbol of transition from one place to another, from one category ('here') to a new category ('over there'). What is true in the world of flesh is true in the world of spirit, and the vision of the Gate can be used for many things.

In this work we use a very simple linear figure as the sigil of the gate. It shows the most ancient and consistent form of door – two upright posts with a lintel placed horizontally atop them. From the trilithons of Stonehenge to the doors of bronze-age mounds; from the temples of Khemi and Athens to the doors of wooden roundhouses in Gaul and Eire, the post-and-lintel is both fact and symbol of the Way Between. When we face the Gate Sigil in vision, we prepare to leave the comfortable fire of our home-mind to enter the wider world. We prepare to leave behind the surface world to go deep into the Mound. We enter the sacred Place of Vision, wherever that may lead us.

There is a traditional occult technique of vision that can handily be applied using this universal symbol. After entering basic trance, the seer envisions a door, portal or curtain, with a particular symbol or image upon it. The symbol is contemplated for a time and then the seer 'passes through' the door or curtain into a locale or experience conditioned by the nature of the symbol. This method is employed later in some of the visions in this series, focused on specific goals. Here we consider the technique in general, widely applicable.

In general it is best to use this method after one has accessed a locale through more formal means. For instance, one could easily choose symbols of the Underworld or Heavens and seek to enter those realms by passing the Gate. This could produce powerful results, but that is more likely when the seer has followed a more literal path into the Underworld, perhaps using the Inner Grove visions in the Fifth Cycle. However many students respond well to the gate method, and it is easy to work for practice and experiment.

The Practice

It can be useful to make a physical representation of the gate sigil. In a Shrine or Temple environment this can mean simply placing a computer image on card or in a frame, and arranging it artfully on the Shrine. The sigil might be drawn on a chalkboard, with whatever additional signs, or the sigil painted permanently and additional signs chalked as needed. In working out-of-doors the sigil might be drawn on a stone or tree with ochre or clay, or scratched in the soil with a wand or staff. Once some skill has been gained the entire work can be done in vision, the sigil simply visualized where desired. In making physical representations of the Gate there is an advantage to using an abstract linear form rather than a more literal or realistic picture of a door. The linear sigil is both simple enough to be drawn anywhere at will and to allow the vision-eye to create detail as needed without conflicting with the sigil's form.

Those working in a Pagan Druidic ritual form may want to arrange the Fire and Well before the sigil. The Gate sigil can then be treated as the visible presence of the ritual Gate, opened in the usual way. As in any vision, some degree of ritual framing helps to establish trance and enhance the power of the work. The simple Grove Hallowing given in the appendix and other places here is sufficient.

The following entrancement uses a simple trick to guide the seer into the Threshold. As always, the script can be recorded, memorized, or simply used a framework for improvisation.

An Entrancement for the Gate Sigil

• *I am seated at the Fire, before the Well... seated at the Open Gate... pause for a moment, and calm my heart... blood and breath and bone... the Druid's Peace...*

• *I open my Inner Eye... Using the Charm of the Open Eye perhaps...*

and stand in my vision body...

• I behold the form of the gate sign... standing before me... growing larger... the post and lintel...

• The Gate is open, but within it is only misty cloud... turning shapelessly... I seek a vision, and so I make the sign of my journey appear in the center of the Gate... focus my awareness on that sign...

• Stepping forward in my vision body, I approach the symbol... and walk into it... and through it... passing through... into the mist...

• The mist is all around me, but I move forward, and once again call upon the sigil of the Gate... and it appears before me... and once again I see the symbol of my journey in the center of the Gate...before me in the mist...

• By will and vision I go to the gate... approach again the symbol... and pass through it... into a landscape of vision... pausing for a moment, the vision becomes clear... mist parting... revealing the Threshold... though I have not yet arrived...

• I move forward through the Threshold... if visions arise, I keep my will clear, and move past them... and before me, as I draw near, I see again the Gate Sign... and in its center the symbol of my journey...

• I know that as I pass this third gate, I will enter the goal of my journey... reach the Inner Threshold of the symbol that I have sought... I approach the Gate... see it clearly and in detail before me... and I focus my attention on the journey symbol... and step through it.

•When I wish to return I once again call the sigil of the Gate before me... post and lintel... and in the space of the gate I see my own shrine... my own hallows...

• Turning my back on my vision, I pass through the Gate again... it may be that I emerge directly into my own place... where my body waits... but if I find myself in the mist, I again open the Gate and pass through... until I arrive at my Fire...

• I turn, and settle my vision eye back into my flesh... and renew my center and my power... seated in the Druid's Peace...

The Hall of Audience
Trance for Invocation

The work of invocation is central to a Pagan relationship with the deities. By making proper offerings, reciting beautiful words and filling our minds with proper images we create an environment into which the influence of the deity flows. In this way we gain the attention of the person of the deity, and bring the mortal self into the presence of the divine.

This is one pattern by which our Druidic sacred space and ritual order can be used for invocation. It centers on the presence of the Gate, a key element in Druidic ritual. If you are adapting these techniques for other Pagan systems, the Gate can be envisioned as a specific element of the trance. I will present a form that mingles stages of trance-vision with stages of actual ritual practice, and then present a direct script that can be worked as the central point of a ritual frame.

Inner Work of the Audience

• Of course in any invocation the Druid should be clear about the symbolism of the deity being called – the proper traditional colors, signs, tools and motifs that surround the figure of the deity. If needed, a series of key visions should be developed before the rite is worked. For those working a Gaelic path there are a set of deity incantations with appropriate visualizations in my book, Draiocht.
• Any rite with a more focused purpose than general worship and blessing should begin with settling into light trance. Beginning with the Bone, Breath and Blood exercise, centering in the Two Powers completes the preparatory work.
• Work the Opening of the Grove in the usual simple form.
• After the honoring of the Three Hallows, and before the Gate Opening, work the Inner Vision technique. The Charm of the Open Eye is proper here:

1: Find your basic trance and abide in it for a moment

2: allow the Mist to arise from you and around you

3: close your material eyes for a time, and drift in the Mist

4: envision your goal, and be drawn toward it

5: draw the Opening Spiral with both material and vision-hand

6: Let the Mist be cleared away, and behold the Threshold vision of your Shrine

7: Open your eyes, and know the Double Sight

When you are skilled in this progression of vision then this short charm can be recited three times, so that the Short Road will be easily remembered as you go.

Between Fire and Water, I find my balance
From the Union of Fire and Water the Mist rises
Let the Mist carry me, and my Eye of Vision open
Let the Eye lead me, and my vision be clear and true
Let my Vision enchant me, with the sorcerer's sight
Eye of Vision, eye of flesh, let me scc clearly
That the Work of the Wise be done.

• Once your Inner Eye is Opened, construct the Vision of the God's Gate:

The Vision of the God's Gate
• *With the Eye open, focus your attention on the presence of the Gate in the center of the Grove.*
• *In whatever way is true for you, let your vision eye see through the open Gate, and there behold the doors of a mighty and beautiful temple, suitable for the God who you are calling.*
• *Perhaps it appears on the front of a full temple, or perhaps it simple drifts in the mist, but it stands firmly closed, and upon the doors are shown the symbols of the God who waits behind it.*
• *Observe what materials compose the doors. Are they locked, or simply standing firm? What signs are graven upon them, and what letters?*
• *Let the image grow clear, as you work the Gate Opening.*

• Make any other preliminary offerings.

The Vision of the Eidolon
• Returning your attention to the envisioned doors of the temple, make an internal or audible call to the deity, saying, perhaps:

O blessed (deity's name) open to me the doors of your vision. Let me see your image, that I may make proper

offering to you.

• *Envision the opening of the doors of the temple. As they open, a kind of light spills out around the enlarging opening... as the doors part... opening wide... to reveal the presence of the perfect image of the God you seek...*

• *See the form of the deity, seated or standing, properly enthroned, or upon a place of honor... See the form of the body — of the robes or clothing or adornment... in colors and style fitting to the nature of the deity... See the symbols proper to the god... borne in the god's hands... or arranged around them... beasts and herbs and flowers and tools...*

• *You glimpse the deity's face, almost invisible in the divine light... Eyes, smile, and the beautiful, calm light of the power of the god...*

• *You gaze at the image, framed in the Gate, and the light of the shining deity fills your vision, the deity's form almost hidden in the dancing light... and you make your offerings, saying:*

• Recite the invocation of the deity, and make the proper offerings.

The Audience

• *With the offerings complete, settle your body and prepare for the vision... breathe deep and renew your relaxation and basic trance... allowing focus to turn away from the outer Shrine to the inner vision...*

• *See again the flowing colored light, shining out of the doors of the inner temple... see again the eidolon of the god... the center of the light...*

• *... and, in response to your offerings and praise, the god stretches forth a hand...*

• *The god is calling, and your vision is drawn in through the doors of the temple... the image of the god grows larger and larger... towering before you... yet reaching out in welcome...*

• *You stand before the god...*

• *Where before the light was like a veil, now it reveals... the form of the deity clear before you... robes, symbols and form... and especially the*

face and eyes of that mighty being...
• *And in that vision you stand in the presence of the god... eyes meet eyes..., and you might speak a Prayer of Audience... saying perhps...*

O shining (deity's name)
Presence of power, light of wisdom, flow of love
Behold me now, as I behold you.
I behold your face – behold you, now, my face.
I behold your hands – behold you, now, my hands.
I behold your shining heart – behold you, now, my heart,
As we abide together in vision.

• *Feel the presence of the deity, and let your own presence be as a mirror... your brow reflecting the face of the god... your hands joining with the hands of the god... your heart like a still pool reflecting the form of the god...*
• *now abide for a time in this vision, speaking as you may with the god...*
• *And when you have finished the Audience, then you may return your awareness again to your material seat, in your shrine...*
• *If it seems proper, envision the doors of the temple closing again... the image of the deity still reflected in your heart... and settle again into your common flesh, prepared to continue the work...*
• Complete your ritual.

Meeting With the Allies (Spirits)

- *Come to your Shrine or Hallows, Bless all and open a gate.*
- *Perform the Nineteen Working, paying good attention to the Da Fein invocation.*
- *Use your Short Road to the Grove:*

Between Fire and Water, I find my balance
From the Union of Fire and Water the Mist rises
Let the Mist carry me, and my Eye of Vision open
Let the Eye lead me, and my vision be clear and true
Let my Vision enchant me, with the sorcerer's sight
Eye of Vision, eye of flesh, let me see clearly
That the Work of the Wise be done.

- *Remember and re-establish the Inner Hallows, and the surrounding environment.*
- *Stand at your Inner Fire, and bring the Two Powers into your vision body... hold up your hands, and know that whatever sacrifice you have given in the common world will also be available to you here in the Threshold... so make your usual offerings to the Hallows, and speak as you will...*
- *Let silver come to your hand... and give it, a substance of yourself, to the Well... and speak in the voice of your vision...*
- *Let precious scented oil come to your hand... and give it, a substance of yourself, to the Fire... and speak in the voice of your vision...*
- *Let burning herbs and pure water come into your two hands... and with them, substance of yourself, honor the Tree, sprinkling its roots and perfuming its leaves... and speak in the voice of your vision...*
- *pause and feel the presence of the place... its weight and solidity... its weirdness and limnality... remember...*
- *First call to your Allies — to the Teacher and Familiar who you have met. If they appear, that is good. If they do not appear immediately, know that they have heard you, and proceed. Take a moment to know the presence of your allies at your sides, in whatever way they manifest to you...*
- *This is your chance to speak with these spirits, to ask your questions and boons... They may speak and act in turn, they may listen and give only*

strange signs, they may not seem to be present in their images at all... but they are in contact with you, because they have promised to be so, and so you should call to them and speak with them...

- Now as you address them, remember to seek their names and signs, their rank and powers and proper offerings, so that you can know them with honor... as you speak with the Allies for a time, in the Inner Grove...

The Return

- Now, as you prepare to finish your work, remember... remember all that you have seen and done... all that you have learned...

- Bid farewell to your Allies, knowing that they will stand by you at your need...

- And, standing in vision in your Grove... remember your body... where it sits before the Hallows in the common world... Look out to the edge of your Grove, and there, see the Gate Sign appear... and the Mist beyond it... walk across the Grove, and pass easily through the Sign, remembering your body as your goal... and step out before your Fire in your common Hallows...

- Remember your Hallows, and see yourself seated there before them... go to your body... turn, and step backward into the space where your body is sitting... raise your spirit-hand before you... and make a tuathal triskel in the air before you... sit down into your body... renew your center... feel the Earth and Sky Powers meeting in your flesh...

-Remember your body, and let your awareness be firmly behind your eyes... feel the air flow in your lungs... the blood course in your veins... remember all you have seen and done in this work... open your eyes, and know that your spirit has returned fully to your flesh... stretch... and be finished with the trance.

A Vision of the Mother of All

Come to your Shrine, open as usual and enter a basic trance. If you wish to open the Gate, do so, then envision the Earth Mother in the Gate:

• See the Mother of All, the Mountain Woman, before you. She is huge as a hill, seated with her back against the World Tree, naked, sitting with her knees drawn up, displaying her cunny and her round belly. Her breasts are great and round, hips and thighs mighty. She holds one hand raised, palm turned toward you, and the other she extends, palm up, as if in offering or receiving. Her face is beautiful, eyes kind and wise, and she smiles lovingly.

• Around her head shines a nimbus of light, gold and silver like sun and moon. Vines and trees are her gown, flowers and fruits her ornaments. Her womb shines and flickers with a light like moonlight on moving water. Every beast and bird, serpent and crawling thing are her court as the green of the world grows all around her. To gaze upon her is to feel the unconditional offer of her bounty, and also her challenge to the strong and to the weak.

Make simple offerings of grain or oil, or as you can, nine times as you recite this hymn three times:

Mighty Mother of All; Womb of Life
Source of Plenty; Soul of the Land
I make due offering to you
(offering given)
Because you uphold the World
Because you freely give your Bounty
Because you grant every Blessing
I make due offering to you
(offering given)
Queen of Sovereignty, I worship your Power
Mother of the Earth, I worship your Bounty
Giver of Every Life
I worship your Spirit
Earth Mother,
uphold my work as you do the world
Earth Mother, accept my sacrifice!

(offering given)

Renew your vision of the Mother, and abide for a while in that vision. Then proceed, thus:

• *Contemplate the wonderful being of the Earth Mother for a time. When her presence feels real to you, envision your own body, seated where you are, as lying within Her Womb. Become aware of your own body, naked beneath your garments. Feel the Mother appear around you, vast, your form an egg among countless eggs, kept safe and warm, filled with potential. Abide for a while in contemplation of this vision.*

• *When you are ready, allow the whole vision, both the Mother and your own form, to shrink down and be enthroned in your own heart. Let the love and power and all-flowing generosity, the safety and strength and warmth be concentrated in you. Feel the presence of the Mother shining in you, within the boundaries of your seated form. Abide for a while in contemplation of this vision.*

• *Finally, allow the image to grow again, until the seed-self is reunited with your material presence. Allow the form of the Mother to grow larger and larger, attenuating to become one with the land around you.*

Renew your center, balancing all once again within you, and recite a simple ending charm, such as:

The blessings of the Holy Ones
be on me and mine
My thanks unto all beings,
with peace on thee and thine
The Fire, the Well, the Sacred Tree
Flow and Flame and Grow in me
Thus do I remember the work of the Wise.

A Vision of the Lord of Wisdom

Let the Druid come before the Shrine, and enter a basic trance. Work a simple opening rite and compose the Vision of the Lord of Wisdom, thus:

• Envision the Lord of Wisdom, the Keeper of Gates, before you. See his towering figure, huge above a crossroad in the mist, feet floating above the road. He is slender and strong, dressed only in an open robe of white that billows in the moving air. His face is youthful, but his long hair and beard are snowy white. His left hand is raised, palm forward, and in his right hand he bears a shining white wand with a flame at its tip.

• Around his head shines a nimbus of every color and pattern, filled with every sign and letter of wisdom, shining around his being. His forehead shines with a wondrous light, with a flickering flame in the center. He stands at the crossroad, and you see that every road of it stretches away to another crossroad, and another. At each the Lord stands, in reflection outward, standing at the Center of All Ways, the Fire at the Center of the World.

Make a simple offering of whiskey or incense, or as you can, nine times, as you recite this hymn three times:

Lord of Wisdom; Wanderer on the Roads
Keeper of Gates and Ways; Priest of the Sacred Grove
I make due offering to you
(Offering given)
Because you teach wisdom
Because you guide spirits
Because you reveal secrets
I make due offering to you
(Offering given)
Lord of the Twilight, I worship your cunning
Keeper of Gates, I worship your might
Teacher of Heroes, I worship your wisdom
Lord of Secret Knowledge,
inspire my mind with the Elder Ways
Keeper of Gates, accept my sacrifice!
(Offering given)

Renew your vision of the Gatekeeper and abide for a while in contemplation of that vision. Then proceed thus:

• Contemplate the shining presence of the Lord of Wisdom for a time. When his presence feels real to you then envision yourself seated at the crossroad with the gatekeeper behind you, his aura surrounding and interpenetrating you. You gaze along the roads and you see yourself at every crossing point, your awareness extending outward along the Infinite Paths. Feel your extending presence, out through the whole Web of Worlds. Abide for a while in contemplation of this vision.

• When you are ready, allow the whole vision, the Gatekeeper, the Web and your own form to shrink down and to become equal to your own head. Let the wisdom, knowledge and cleverness, the freedom to pass every barrier be concentrated in you. Feel the presence of the Gatekeeper shining in you, within the boundaries of your seated form. Abide for a while in contemplation of this vision.

• Finally, allow the image to grow again, bringing all the reflections of yourself firmly together in your material presence. Allow the form of the Gatekeeper to grow larger and larger, attenuating to become one with the light and air.

Renew your center, balancing all once again within you, and recite a simple ending charm, such as:

The blessings of the Holy Ones
be on me and mine
My blessings on all beings,
with peace on thee and thine
The Fire, the Well, the Sacred Tree
Flow and Flame and Grow in me
Thus do I remember the work of the Wise.

A Cosmos Vision

• *Breathe deep, and let your body settle in its place... shake out your arms... let your shoulders relax and drop... and focus, for a moment, on your breath... begin your breathing pattern... in... and out... and, as you breathe, remember the feeling of deep physical relaxation... let the feeling flow in your flesh... as you focus on your breathing pattern... your legs relax... and your arms... your torso, and your shoulders... as you turn your awareness inward, and focus on your pattern of breathing...*

• *Now, as the chime sounds the count, bring the Two Powers into yourself... by breath and by will, as the chime sounds...*
(chime rung for the Nine Breaths Centering)

• *And so the Shadow and the Light are in you... the strengthening Waters and the transforming Fire... focusing your attention inward... with the Two Powers flowing and shining, you are like the Center of the Sacred Grove... let the Hearth of the Fire be in your heart... let the Font of the Waters be in your loins... feel your roots deep below, and your crown spreading high... like the Tree of All-That-Is...*

• *Now, as the Tree grows in you, you can feel yourself begin to grow larger... feel your head rise and your shoulders widen... your form is insubstantial, as you grow in vision... your perspective rising from your place in the common world... through your roof... above trees... away from the common world... You reach a point when you step growing larger... now, in this form, you choose to stand... your vision rising again, from where you sit... to stand tall, in the Center of the Worlds...*
• *where you stand, turn in place, and let your vision see far... in this work, it will not be enough to see in only one direction... just as the Light of your Inner Fire shines in all directions, so you must open your awareness to the full sphere of your existence... and so, with your vision made full circle, let your awareness reach out to the Land on which you stand...*

• *Become aware that you stand in the center of the World of the Land...
let your vision range out, from the places around you, which you know
well... to the features of nearby lands... to all the world of Land...
to the huge and ancient strengths of deep earth, that move the face of
the planet... to stone and mountains and rivers, plains and meadows...
swamps and deserts, forests and jungles... and everywhere upon it, the
works of living things... the dwellings of uncounted beings... from the
tiniest eaters of soil to the great beasts... and the works of humankind...*

• *As your vision expands, you see that the Land is surrounded and contained
within the World of the Sea... the Land reaches its end, in deltas and
cliffs and beaches, and the Sea rolls out, even as the waves roll in... at
first the Sea may be blue and warm, or it may pound grey upon stones...
but after the ninth wave, as your awareness expands in all directions, the
Sea becomes the Great Deep... vast and empty on its face, teeming with
strange life in the depths... a few tiny ships upon its surface... away into
the distance the Sea stretches... at its edge the Sea fades into mist... a
swirling grey chaos, in which vague forms swirl and vanish...*
• *Your vision rises from the edges of the Sea... from the unknown
boundary... and into the World of the Sky as you continue to expand and
enlarge... you know, first, the air — the realm between the tree-tops and
the highest clouds... the realm of birds and flying things, of storm and
wind and the flows of weather... and, above the air, the great lights of
the Heavens... in the black void outside the air shine the Sun and Moon,
ever turning in their stately dance... in the center of the Sky stands the
Nail of the Heavens — the Pole Star... and around it wheel the stars, in
their eternal pattern...*

• *Now, in your vision, you encompass all of the Middle Realm... firm
upon the Land, the Sea all around you... the sky about your head... yet
you know that this is only the surface of the world... and that you must
open to the secret and Inner Worlds...*

• *Breathe deep, and let your breath carry your vision... in your midst you remember the Hallows of the Center... the Tree of Worlds, the Altar of the Fire in which the Sacred Flame burns, and the Holy Well of the Water that rises from the Deep...*

• *You begin by following the Waters... let your awareness be full of the Power of the Deep, and let your vision Eye enter the Well at the Center... merging with the Waters, flowing down and beyond the Middle World, into the Deep... down... among the roots of the World Tree... past stone and skull, and the small beings that eat the dead... into the moist dark...*

• *And you become aware that beneath the surface of things there opens the whole of the Under World — the Realm of the Deep... you see the rolling forests and plains of the Land beneath... lit by their own light, without Sun or Moon... the whole of the Under Land shining in a riot of color and changing form...*
• *In the Center stand the Underworld Hallows... the Fire, Well and Tree as they appear in this place... and the Underworld, filled with the spirits who dwell here... broad and varied, surrounded by its own Sea, as it fades at the edges to a dark and roiling mist... which you know is connected, in some way, with the mist at the edge of the empty Sea...*

• *In this Deep Realm dwell the Hosts of the Dead... our Ancestors of blood and heart and spirit... all pursuing their fates as Fate leads... there dwell the Underworld Gods... with their powers of growth and decay, wealth and wild wisdom... here lie many places of mystery and wonder, and it may be that you will wander here, in time... but for now, pause for a moment, and experience the vision of the Underworld from your place at the Center...*

• *Now, remember the Center, and let your vision return to the Underworld Tree... at its base bubbles a well that murmers of deeper places... at* its base stands an altar of black stone, on which burns the Fire of the Sky, even here... you know that far above you the leaves of the Tree are receiving the Light of the Heavens... that even here the roots of the Tree shine dark with that Light...

• Your Vision Eye can rise on that Light, along the trunk of the World Tree... following the spark up into the branches and leaves... rising from the Deep, through the Middle World... even past the Sky... and into a vision of light and pattern and sound... where all things are bright, even in their shadows, and all is one great pattern of connection...

• In the Realm of the Heavens, the Great dance proceeds... the Great Lights, the stars and planets, the living and the non-living, making together the Eternal Pattern of all things... in the Center stand the Hallows of the heavens... the Fire, Well and Tree as they appear in this place... a pure crystal altar, from which shines a perfect Light, a Fountain of flowing Shadow... a Pillar-Tree with roots of iron and leaves of precious stone... and around the Hallows, the Heavens dance...

• As you gaze out at the Realm of the Heavens, the dance of pattern and light resolves into landscape... rolling meadows and trees, streams and pools beneath a shining, patterned sky... upon the hilltops stand the temples of the Gods of the Heavens... and the hosts of their servants and messengers... shining, perhaps winged...

• Now let your attention return to the High Hallows... to the Heaven Fire on its crystal altar... to the fountain of color that brings the Deep Shadow even to this realm... to the Tree of Jewels... whose branches arch over all existence... shining the Light into the Worlds...

• The Light shines down into the Middle World... onto the Land and Sea and Sky... and you see that the rainbow flows of the Underworld Power rise up there as well... and in the Two Powers, as they flow in the Middle

World, you behold the Spirits, the clans of Otherworldly beings who dwell in the living world... animal and vegetable spirits, and the souls of stones and streams... secret halls beneath the hills, and on the high places, beings of pools and winds and the dark corners of cities... the spirit kindreds of the Middle Realm...

• Now you have built the vision of the Threefold World of the Druids... let your awareness expand again... to contain this whole pattern... remember the Sacred Center... the Fire, Well and Tree here in your Grove, that reach from the Underworld to the Heavens... that stand in the Center as in the Center of All Worlds... remember the Underworld, and its dark rainbow... remember the Heavens in their shining... and the Middle Realm... land, Sea and Sky... both their material forms and beings, and the hosts of Midrealm spirits... the Landwights... and in the Underworld, the Mighty Dead... and in the Heavens, the Shining Gods... and all these beings moving between all the worlds... a flow of wisdom love and power... in all that is...

• Rest now in this vision... feel and see and know it... breathe deep... your breath flows, and the cosmos flows... ... ...

• Breathe deep... and remember... remember this vision... as the time comes to return... remember your body... and allow your awareness to contract... to draw inward... into your flesh, into your common mind... breathe deep, and feel the Two Powers in your flesh... and remember... as your awareness returns, calm and refreshed... filled with the Vision of the Cosmos... to your common form... and you open your eyes...

Made in the USA
Lexington, KY
29 August 2015